Multilingual Multi-document Summarization

(MultiLing 2013)

Sofia, Bulgaria
9 August 2013

ISBN: 978-1-62748-994-2

Printed from e-media with permission by:

Curran Associates, Inc.
57 Morehouse Lane
Red Hook, NY 12571

Some format issues inherent in the e-media version may also appear in this print version.

Printed by Curran Associates, Inc. (2013)

Association for Computational Linguistics
209 N. Eighth Street
Stroudsburg, Pennsylvania 18360

Phone: 1-570-476-8006
Fax: 1-570-476-0860

acl@aclweb.org

Additional copies of this publication are available from:

Curran Associates, Inc.
57 Morehouse Lane
Red Hook, NY 12571 USA
Phone: 845-758-0400
Fax: 845-758-2634
Email: curran@proceedings.com
Web: www.proceedings.com

MultiLing 2013

MultiLing 2013: Multilingual Multi-document Summarization

Proceedings of the Workshop

August 9, 2013
Sofia, Bulgaria

Introduction

MultiLing 2013 is a community effort, a set of research tasks and a corresponding workshop which covers three subdomains of Natural Language Processing, focused on the multilingual aspect of summarization. Each domain is allocated a separate section of the workshop. The three domains are:

- Multilingual multi-document summarization: Summarization, especially from multiple documents, has received increasing attention during the last years. This is mostly due to the increasing volume and redundancy of available online information. Recently, more and more interest arises for methods that will be able to function on a variety of languages. Multilingual multi-document summarization is the domain that researches such methods and studies their requirements and intricacies.
- Multilingual summary evaluation: Summary evaluation has been an open question for several years, even though there exist methods that correlate well to human judgment, when called upon to compare systems. In the multilingual setting, it is not obvious that these methods will perform equally well to the English language setting. In fact, some preliminary results have shown that several problems may arise in the multilingual setting [1]. This section of the workshop aims to cover and discuss these research problems and corresponding solutions.
- Multilingual summarization data collection and exploitation: The collection of multi-lingual corpora for summarization and summarization evaluation offers a challenge in itself. This section of the workshop works towards well-defined practices for the collection of such data, as well as the implementation and use of community tools for the support of the collection process. Furthermore, this section will include a discussion on how we can maximize the effect of the generated corpora in favor or the scientific community.

References

[1] Giannakopoulos, G., El-Haj, M., Favre, B., Litvak, M., Steinberger, J., and Varma, V. (2011). TAC2011 MultiLing Pilot Overview.

Organizers:

George Giannakopoulos, NCSR "Demokritos" (Greece)
Georgios Petasis, NCSR "Demokritos" (Greece)

Program Committee:

Hoa Trang Dang, NIST (USA)
Lucy Vanderwende, Microsoft (USA)
Horacio Saggion, Universitat Pompeu Fabra (Spain)
Vangelis Karkaletsis, NCSR "Demokritos" (Greece)
Karolina Owczarzak, Oracle (USA)
John Conroy, IDA Center for Computing Sciences (USA)
George Giannakopoulos, NCSR "Demokritos" (Greece)

Invited Speaker:

Dragomir R. Radev, University of Michigan, Ann Arbor (USA)

Table of Contents

Conference Program

Friday August 9, 2013

09:00 Introduction by the Organizers

Session 1: (09:05) Data Contribution and Exploitation

09:05 *Multi-document multilingual summarization corpus preparation, Part 1: Arabic, English, Greek, Chinese, Romanian*
Lei Li, Corina Forascu, Mahmoud El-Haj and George Giannakopoulos

09:35 *Multi-document multilingual summarization corpus preparation, Part 2: Czech, Hebrew and Spanish*
Michael Elhadad, Sabino Miranda-Jiménez, Josef Steinberger and George Giannakopoulos

Session 2: (10:05) Multi-document Summarization

10:05 *Multi-document multilingual summarization and evaluation tracks in ACL 2013 MultiLing Workshop*
George Giannakopoulos

10:30 Coffee break

11:00 *ACL 2013 MultiLing Pilot Overview*
Jeff Kubina, John Conroy and Judith Schlesinger

11:30 *CIST System Report for ACL MultiLing 2013 – Track 1: Multilingual Multi-document Summarization*
Lei Li, Wei Heng, Jia Yu, Yu Liu and Shuhong Wan

11:50 *Multilingual Multi-Document Summarization with POLY2*
Marina Litvak and Natalia Vanetik

12:10 *The UWB Summariser at Multiling-2013*
Josef Steinberger

12:30 Lunch break

14:00 Invited Talk: Natural Language Processing for Analyzing Collective Discourse, Dragomir R. Radev, University of Michigan

15:00 *Multilingual Summarization: Dimensionality Reduction and a Step Towards Optimal Term Coverage*
John Conroy, Sashka T. Davis, Jeff Kubina, Yi-Kai Liu, Dianne P. O'Leary and Judith D Schlesinger

Friday August 9, 2013 (continued)

15:30	Coffee break
16:00	*Using a Keyness Metric for Single and Multi Document Summarisation* Mahmoud El-Haj and Paul Rayson
	Session 3: (16:20) Single-document Summarization
16:20	*Multilingual summarization system based on analyzing the discourse structure at MultiLing 2013* Daniel Anechitei and Eugen Ignat
16:40	*Multilingual Single-Document Summarization with MUSE* Marina Litvak and Mark Last
17:00	Closing Discussion

Multi-document multilingual summarization corpus preparation, Part 1: Arabic, English, Greek, Chinese, Romanian

Lei Li
BUPT, China
leili@bupt.edu.cn

Corina Forascu
RACAI, Romania
UAIC, Romania
corinfor@info.uaic.ro

Mahmoud El-Haj
Lancaster Univ., UK
m.el-haj@lancaster.ac.uk

George Giannakopoulos
NCSR Demokritos, Greece
SciFY NPC, Greece
ggianna@iit.demokritos.gr

Abstract

This document overviews the strategy, effort and aftermath of the MultiLing 2013 multilingual summarization data collection. We describe how the Data Contributors of MultiLing collected and generated a multilingual multi-document summarization corpus on 10 different languages: Arabic, Chinese, Czech, English, French, Greek, Hebrew, Hindi, Romanian and Spanish. We discuss the rationale behind the main decisions of the collection, the methodology used to generate the multilingual corpus, as well as challenges and problems faced per language. This paper overviews the work on Arabic, Chinese, English, Greek, and Romanian languages. A second part, covering the remaining languages, is available as a distinct paper in the MultiLing 2013 proceedings.

1 Introduction

Summarization has recently received the focus of media attention (Cahan, 2013; Shih, 2013), due to a set of corporate buy-outs related to summarization technology companies. This trend of applying summarization is the result of a long research effort related to summarization. Previously, especially within the Text Analysis Conference (TAC) series of workshops (Dang, 2005; Dang, 2006; Dang and Owczarzak, 2008), multi-document summarization has covered aspects of summarization such as update summarization, guided summarization and cross-lingual summarization. In TAC 2011 the MultiLing Pilot (Giannakopoulos et al., 2011) was introduced: a combined community effort to present and promote multi-document summarization apporaches that are (fully or partly) language-neutral. To support this effort an organizing committee across more than six countries was assigned to create a multi-lingual corpus on news texts, covering seven different languages: Arabic, Czech, English, French, Greek, Hebrew, Hindi.

The Pilot gave birth to an active community of researchers, who provided the effort and know-how to realize a continuation of the original effort: MultiLing 2013. The MultiLing 2013 Workshop, taking place within ACL 2013, built upon the existing corpus of MultiLing 2011 to provide additional languages and challenges for summarization systems. This year 3 new languages were added: Chinese, Romanian and Spanish. Furthermore, more texts were added to most existing corpus languages (with the exception of French and Hindi).

In the following paragraphs we first overview the MultiLing tasks, for which the corpus was built (Section 2). We then describe the rationale and strategy applied for the corpus collection and creation (Section 3). We continue with special comments for the English, Greek, Chinese and Romanian languages (Section 4). Finally, we summarize the findings at the end of this paper (Section 5). We note that a second paper (Elhadad et al., 2013) describes the language-specific notes related to the rest of the MultiLing 2013 language contributions (Czech, Hebrew, Spanish).

2 The MultiLing tasks

There are two main tasks (and a single-document multilingual summarization pilot described in a separate paper) in MultiLing 2013:

Summarization Task This MultiLing task aims to evaluate the application of (partially or fully) language-independent summarization algorithms on a variety of languages. Each system participating in the task was called to provide summaries for a range of different languages, based on corresponding corpora. In the MultiLing Pilot of 2011 the languages used were 7, while this year systems were called to summarize texts in 10 different languages: Arabic, Chinese, Czech, English, French, Greek, Hebrew, Hindi, Romanian, Spanish. Participating systems were required to apply their methods to a minimum of two languages.

The task was aiming at the real problem of summarizing news topics, parts of which may be described or may happen in different moments in time. We consider, similarly to MultiLing 2011(Giannakopoulos et al., 2011) that news topics can be seen as *event sequences*:

Definition 1 *An event sequence is a set of atomic (self-sufficient) event descriptions, sequenced in time, that share main actors, location of occurence or some other important factor. Event sequences may refer to topics such as a natural disaster, a crime investigation, a set of negotiations focused on a single political issue, a sports event.*

The summarization task requires to generate a single, fluent, representative summary from a set of documents describing an event sequence. The language of the document set will be within the given range of 10 languages and all documents in a set share the same language. The output summary should be of the same language as its source documents. The output summary should be between 240 and 250 words.

Evaluation Task This task aims to examine how well automated systems can evaluate summaries from different languages. This task takes as input the summaries generated from automatic systems and humans in the Summarization Task. The output should be a grading of the summaries. Ideally, we would want the automatic evaluation to maximally correlate to human judgement.

The first task was aiming at the real problem of summarizing news topics, parts of which may be described or happen in different moments in time. The implications of including multiple aspects of the same event, as well as time relations at a varying level (from consequtive days to years), are still difficult to tackle in a summarization context. Furthermore, the requirement for multilingual applicability of the methods, further accentuates the difficulty of the task.

The second task, summarization evaluation has come to be a prominent research problem, based on the difficulty of the summary evaluation process. While commonly used methods build upon a few human summaries to be able to judge automatic summaries (e.g., (Lin, 2004; Hovy et al., 2005)), there also exist works on fully automatic evaluation of summaries, without human "model" summaries (Louis and Nenkova, 2012; Saggion et al., 2010). The Text Analysis Conference has a separate track, named AESOP (Dang and Owczarzak, 2009) aiming to test and evaluate different automatic evaluation methods of summarization systems.

Given the tasks, a corpus needed to be generated, that would be able to:

- provide input texts in different languages to summarization systems.
- provide model summaries in different languages as gold standard summaries, to also allow for automatic evaluation using model-dependent methods.
- provide human grades to automatic and human summaries in different languages, to support the testing of summary evaluation systems.

In the following section we show how these requirements were met in MultiLing 2013.

3 Corpus collection and generation

The overall process of creating the corpus of MultiLing 2013 was, similarly to MultiLing 2011, based on a community effort. The main processes consisting of the generation of the corpus are as follows:

- Selection of a source corpus in a single language (see Section 3.1).
- Translation of the source corpus to different languages (see Section 3.2).
- Human summarization of corpus topics per language (see Section 3.3).
- Evaluation of human summaries, as well as of submitted system runs (see Section 3.4).

We should note here that the translation is meant to provide a parallel corpus of texts across different languages. The main ideas behind this first approach are that:

- the corpus will allow performing secondary studies, related to the human summarization effort in different languages. Having a parallel corpus is such cases can prove critical, in that it provides a common working base.
- we may be able to study topic-related or domain-related summarization difficulty across languages.
- the parallel corpus highlights language-specific problems (such as ambiguity in word meaning, named entity representation across languages).
- the parallel corpus fixes the setting in which methods can show their cross-language applicability. Examining significantly varying results in different languages over a parallel corpus offers some background on how to improve existing methods and may highlight the need for language-specific resources.

On the other hand, the significant organizational and implementaion effort required for the translation (please see per language notes in the corresponding sections) may lead to a comparable (vs. parallel) corpus in future MultiLing endeavours.

Given the tasks at hand, the Contributors first performed the selection of the texts that would be used for the MultiLing tracks, as described below.

3.1 Selecting the corpus

To support the summarization task, we needed a dataset of freely available news texts (to allow reuse), covering news topics that would contain event sequences. Based on the — apparently good — decisions of the MultiLing 2011 Pilot, we determined that each event sequence in the corpus should contain at least three distinct atomic events, to imply an underlying story.

The dataset created was based on the WikiNews site[1], which covers a variety of news topics, while allowing the reuse of the texts based on the Creative Commons Licence. An example topic with two sample texts derived from the original WikiNews documents is provided in Figure 1. It can be seen clearly that the event in the example has significantly different aspects, since an earthquake caused a radiation leak, via a series of interactions in the real world. Systems would normally be expected to express both aspects of the event with adequate information.

During the selection of the source texts, we first gathered an English corpus of 15 topics (10 of which were already available from MultiLing 2011), each containing 10 texts. We made sure that each topic contained at least one event sequence. From the original HTML text we only kept unformatted content text, without any images, tables or links.

While choosing topics we made sure that there existed topics:

- with varying time granularity. Some topics happen within days (e.g., sports events), while others within years (e.g., Iranian nuclear policy and international negotiations).
- covering various domains. There existed topics related to international politics, sports, natural disasters, political campaigns and elections.
- with a varying number of apparent actors. Some topics focus on specific individuals (e.g., campaign of Barack Obama) while others refer to numerous participants (e.g., para-Olympics and participating athletes).
- with numeric aspects, that would change over time. Such examples are natural disasters (with the number of estimated victims, or the estimated magnitude of earthquakes) and sports events (number of medals per country).
- with an important time dimension. For example during the Egyptian riots, the order of events is non-trivial to determine from text. Determining the order of events is also very challenging while following multi-day sports events. Ignoring the time dimension in such topics is expected to worsen the performance of summarization systems.

Given the English texts, we now needed to provide corresponding texts in all the languages used in MultiLing. To this end, we organized a translation process, which is elaborated below.

[1]See `http://www.wikinews.org`.

Fukushima reactor suffers multiple fires, radiation leak confirmed

Tuesday, March 15, 2011

Fires broke out at the Fukushima Daiichi plant's No. 4 reactor in Japan on Tuesday, according to the Tokyo Electric Power Company. The first fire caused a leak of concentrated radioactive material, according to the Japanese prime minister, Naoto Kan.

The first fire broke out at 9:40 a.m. local time on Tuesday, and was thought to have been put out, but another fire was discovered early on Wednesday, believed to have started because the earlier one had not been fully extinguished.

In a televised statement, the prime minister told residents near the plant that "I sincerely ask all citizens within the 20 km distance from the reactor to leave this zone." He went on to say that "[t]he radiation level has risen substantially. The risk that radiation will leak from now on has risen."

Kan warned residents to remain indoors and to shut windows and doors to avoid radiation poisoning.

The French Embassy in Japan reports that the radiation will reach Tokyo in 10 hours, with current wind speeds.

Death toll rises from Japan quake

Sunday, March 13, 2011

The death toll from the earthquake and subsequent tsunami that hit Japan on Friday has risen to more than a thousand, with many people still missing, according to reports issued over the weekend.

While Japan's police says that only 637 are confirmed dead, media reports say that over a thousand people have been killed, with several hundred bodies still being transported. Thousands more are still unaccounted for; in the town of Minamisanriku, Miyagi Prefecture alone, up to 10,000 people are missing. Four trains that were on the coast have yet to be located.

In the aftermath of the disaster, evacuations of around 300,000 people have taken place; more evacuations are likely in the wake of concerns over a damaged nuclear power plant. According to Prime Minister Naoto Kan, around 3,000 people have been rescued thus far. 50,000 troops from the Japanese military have been deployed to assist in rescue efforts.

The tsunami generated by the quake has destroyed communities along Japan's Pacific coast, with up to 90% of the houses in some towns having been destroyed; at least 3,400 structures have been destroyed in total. Fires have also sprung up among the impacted areas.

Figure 1: Topic Sample (Japan Earthquake and Nuclear Threat)

3.2 Translating the corpus

The English texts selected in the selection step were translated using a sentence-by-sentence approach to each of the other languages: Arabic, Chinese, Czech, French, Greek, Hebrew, Hindi, Romanian, Spanish. This year there was no support for the Hindi and French languages, which still contain 10 topics. Also the Chinese language covers 10 topics. All the remaining languages cover 15 topics.

During the translation process, the guidelines were minimal:

> Given the source language text A, the translator is requested to translate each *sentence* in A, into the target language. Each target sentence should keep the meaning from the source language.

Some additional, optional guidelines (provided in the Appendix) were provided by the Romanian language Contributors, proposing ways to react to date formatting, name translations, etc.

During the translation process, the translators were also asked to keep track of the time spent on different stages of the process: first full reading of the source document, translation and verification.

The whole set of translated documents together with the original English document set will be referred to as the *Source Document Set*. Given the creation process, the Source Document Set contains a total of 1350 texts (vs. 700 from MultiLing 2011): 7 languages with 15 topics per language, 10 texts per topic for a total of 1050 texts; 3 languages with 10 topics per language, 10 texts per topic for a total of 300 texts.

This Source Document Set was provided to participating systems as input for their summarization systems. It was also provided to human summarizers, so that they would provide human, model summaries on each topic and each language. The human summarization process is described in the following section.

3.3 Summarizing topics

In the summarization step of the corpus creation different summarizers were asked to generate one summary per topic in each language. The following guidelines were provided to help the summarizers:

> The summarizer will read the whole set of texts at least once. Then, the summarizer should compose a summary, with *a minimum size of 240 and a maximum size of 250 words*. The summary should be in the same language as the texts in the set. The aim is to create a summary that covers all the major points of the document set (what is major is left to summarizer discretion). The summary should be written using fluent, easily readable language. No formatting or other markup should be included in the text. The output summary should be a self-sufficient, clearly written text, providing no other information than what is included in the source documents.

After summarization, human evaluation was performed. The evaluation covered human summaries, but also summarization system submissions. The details are provided in the following paragraphs.

3.4 Evaluating the summaries

The evaluation of summaries was performed both automatically and manually. The manual evaluation was based on the Overall Responsiveness (Dang and Owczarzak, 2008) of a text, as described below, and the automatic evaluation used the ROUGE (Lin, 2004) and AutoSummENG-MeMoG (Giannakopoulos et al., 2008; Giannakopoulos and Karkaletsis, 2011) and NPowER (Giannakopoulos and Karkaletsis, 2013) methods to provide a grading of performance.

For the manual evaluation the human evaluators were provided the following guidelines:

> Each summary is to be assigned an integer grade from 1 to 5, related to the overall responsiveness of the summary. We consider a text to be worth a 5, if it appears to cover all the important aspects of the corresponding document set using fluent, readable language. A text should be assigned a 1, if it is either unreadable, nonsensical, or contains only trivial information from the document set. We consider the content and the quality of the language to be equally important in the grading.

As indicated in the task, the acceptable limits for the word count of a summary were between 240 and 250 words[2] (inclusive). In the case of Chinese there was a problem determining the number of words. Based on the model summaries gathered we (arbitrarily) set the upper limit of length in *bytes* of the UTF8-encoded summary files to 750 bytes.

4 Language specific notes

In the following paragraphs we provide language-specific overviews related to the corpus contribution effort. The aim of these overviews is to provide a reusable pool of knowledge for future similar efforts.

In this document we elaborate on Arabic, English, Greek, Chinese and Romanian languages. A second document (Elhadad et al., 2013) elaborates on the rest of the languages.

4.1 Arabic language

The preparation of the Arabic corpus for the 2013 MultiLing Summarization tasks was organised jointly by Lancaster University and the University of Essex in the United Kingdom. 20 people participated in translating the English corpus into Arabic, validating the translation and summarising the set of related Arabic articles. The participants are studying, or have finished a university degree in an Arabic speaking country. The participants' age ranged between 21 and 32 years old.

The participants translated the English dataset into Arabic. For each translated article another translator validated the translation and fixed any errors. For each of the translated articles, three manual summaries were created by three different participants (human peers). Amid the summarisation process the participants evaluated the quality of the generated summary by assigning a score between one (unreadable summary) and five (fluent and readable summary). No self evaluation was allowed.

The average time for reading the English news articles by the Arabic native speaker participants was 5.58 minutes. The average time it took them to translate these articles into Arabic was 42.18 minutes and to validate each of the translated Arabic articles the participants took 5.25 minutes on average.

For the summarisation task the average time for reading the set of related articles (10 articles per each set) was 34.44 minutes. The average time for summarising each set was 25.41 minutes.

4.1.1 Problems and Challenges

Many difficulties arose during the creation of the gold-standard summaries. Some are language-dependent and relate to the complexity of the Arabic language. This required a special attention to be paid while creating the summaries.

One problem concerns the handling of month names in Arabic. There are two ways of translating month names into Arabic:

- using the Arabic transliteration of the Aramic (Syriac) month names (e.g. "*May*", "أَيَّار", "Ayyar").
- using the Arabic transliteration of the English month names (e.g. "*May*", "مَايُو", "Mayo").

Some of the participants found it difficult to translate sentences where they believe they contain an ambiguous structure. For example: "She said Iranian security Chief Saeed Jalili had requested a meeting in a telephone call" . The translators (who are Native Arabic speakers) found it a bit hard to choose between two translations:

- "Saeed Jalili asked to schedule a telephone meeting"
- "Saeed Jalili phoned to request a meeting" .

Arabic sentence structure is highly complex and therefore great attention must be paid when moving forward or pushing back phrases within a sentence, as such shifts are likely to change the overall meaning. In addition, the use of passive voice, metaphors and idioms in the original English text has captured the translators attention, as the meaning in such cases takes precedence over the literal translation.

During the summarisation process, a summariser found that ordering a set of related articles (discussing the same topic) in chronological order simplifies the summarisation process.

Many participants found it difficult to meet the 250 summary word-limit as they believe 250 is not enough to cover all the essential information derived from a given set of documents.

Another problem concerns 'proper nouns' when translating into Arabic. The Arabic electronic discourse would sometimes show two variants of one

[2] The count of words was provided by the *wc -w* linux command.

English proper noun, as in the case with the name 'Francois Hollande'. Mostly in such cases, the variant used in popular websites such as the Arabic version Wikipedia was adopted.

Finally, there were many questions by the participants on whether to create abstractive or extractive summaries.

4.2 Chinese language

Below we provide an overview of the organizational effort and comments on a variety of problems related to the preparation of the Chinese corpus for MultiLing 2013.

4.2.1 Organization

First, the Chinese language team translated two texts from English to Chinese together in order to make an original unified example for each translator, including file format, title format, date format, named entity translation, etc. Second, we assigned different set of news texts as specific task for each translator. For each news topic, we usually split the ten texts to two different translators at least, so as to bring more thoughts from different viewers and prepare enough for later discussion. During the process of each translator, they were asked to note any problems in a 'problem file', including the source English part and the target Chinese part. Third, we summed up a big problem file from each translator. After a series of discussions, we classified the problems into different categories and solved some of the problems successfully. The remaining problems were noted down in a detailed report to the organizer of the MultiLing 2013 Workshop of ACL 2013, as a knowledge pool for future efforts. Fourth, we performed the verification task. During the process, we made sure that for each text, the verifier was different from the translator. Also each verifier was demanded to log any problems. Fifth, we did another discussion for new problems coming from the verification phase. Some problems were solved; others were added to the detailed report. Sixth, we generated the needed result files and made sure that they were in the requested format (e.g., UTF8, no-BOM, plain text files for summaries).

For the process of summarization and human evaluation, first, we assigned three summarizers, each of which needed to read all the ten topics and write a summary for each topic. Second, we assigned three evaluators, making sure that for each summary, the evaluator was different from the summarizer. Third, we made a discussion about the process of summarization and evaluation. All agreed that summarization and evaluation were much easier than translation.

There were mainly two common problems. One was about the summary length. So we set a unified method for length checking. The other problem was more complex, which was that there were many different information in the original ten texts, but the result summary was limited to 250 words, so it was very difficult to choose the most important information. As a result, some information could be lost in final summaries. At the same time, we also found minor problems regarding the translation, improved the translation files and updated the detailed report about the problems we faced.

4.2.2 Problems and proposed solutions

In fact, related problems mainly came up from the task of translation. Most of them were common questions of the translators and language-dependent problems that needed special care. Here we only list the main categories of problems [3]. First, there were problems with the translation of person names. There are several sub-problems here:

- There are some person names which are not so popular, we could not find a result, so we finally keep the unknown English words among Chinese words.
- There is no specific separator between first name, middle name and family name in English, only normal space. But in Chinese, we usually add a separator "· " between them.
- There is also some ambiguity in person name to us, since we may be not quite familiar with some specific knowledge of news related domain.
- There are also some person names which seem to contain non-English characters. These names are more difficult for us, so we just keep most of them as the original format in English news.
- There are some person names with only one capitalized character and a dot in the middle

[3] A more detailed report has been submitted to the organizer of the Workshop.

part. It' s really difficult for us to find a corresponding Chinese translation for it, so we just keep it as the original English format in the Chinese translations and keep the original English name in the following brackets.

Second, the translation for the English name of some websites, companies, organizations, etc, can cause problems. Since the full name may be too long for news reports, most of them also have occurred in corresponding simple format of abbreviation. Some of them are famous enough that we have a popular Chinese translation for them, while others are not so popular. So we decided that for unknown ones, we just reserve the English name, but for those known ones, we add the Chinese translation and keep some of the English abbreviation.

Third, the translation of time expressions is nontrivial. In English, the order usually used is: Weekday, Month Day, Year. But according to Chinese habit, we mention time usually in the following order: Year Month Day, Weekday.

Fourth, translation of locations names may not exist. There are many location names in these news texts. We tried to find their Chinese translation from many resources, but there are still some difficult ones left.

Fifth, there are some English words in the source texts which seem to be unrelated to other sentences in the news text (these may be text captions of photos in the source WikiNews articles). We just left them as they were.

Sixth, there are some sentences which are difficult to understand clearly because the context and structure are ambiguous. In these cases, we made a Chinese translation which seems best to us.

The above problems conclude the Chinese language contribution language-specific notes.

4.3 English and Greek languages

The effort related to the organization of the English and Greek languages was essentially equivalent to the MultiLing 2011 pilot (Giannakopoulos et al., 2011). This year 5 new topics were added to the two languages. The effort for English was reduced because no translation was needed. In the following subsections we elaborate on the organization details and the problems faced during the different subprocesses of the corpus creation.

4.3.1 Organization

A total of 7 people (being either MSc students, or researchers, all with fluency in English and Greek) were recruited for the two languages. An initial meeting was held to provide the basic guidelines and discuss questions on the translation process. Subsequently, e-mail communication and periodic conferences were used to assign the next tasks, related to summarization and evaluation.

For the purposes of meaningful assignment we created and used an automatic assignment script, that allows pre-allocating specific texts to workers (for any of the required tasks), while it automatically distributes work according to the availability of workers. The script avoids assigning workers to texts/tasks more than once.

In the evaluation process, we made sure (through pre-assignments) that no human would judge their own summary. It would have increased efficiency, if we had ascertained that human summarization would occur right after the translation of the texts.

The average time for reading the English news articles by the Greek native speaker participants was around 8 minutes. The average time it took them to translate these articles into Greek was around 48 minutes on average (with a couple of extreme cases exceeding 100 minutes, due to technical terminology, which was difficult to translate). The summarization time of the new topics in English was around 24 minutes per topic (plus an average of 8 minutes allocated to reading the source texts). For Greek the summary time was around 50 minutes per topic (we note that the summarizers' groups for English and Greek were only minimally overlapping). In the Greek case, some deeper search showed that a single summarizer heavily biased the distribution of times to higher values.

To follow the progress of tasks, a generic project management tool was used. However, the tool proved insufficient in the micro-planning of the effort (individual assignments tracking). It would clearly make sense to use an ad-hoc designed system for planning and implementation of the effort.

4.3.2 Problems and proposed solutions

The main problems identified by contributors for Greek and English translation were related to well-known translation problems: named entity translation, date formatting, highly technical or domain specific terminology, ambiguous terms in the source text. Additional effort from translators provided solutions to these problems according to common practice in the translation domain.

The summarization effort indicated a few interesting points. Even though summarizers have their individual method for summarizing, some common practices and notes arise:

- A non-thorough glimpse of the source texts helps determine the overall topic.
- Time ordering is important in several cases, thus time ordering of the source texts is applied before the summarization process itself. The process is non-trivial even for humans.
- An initial summary which may be longer than the target size is created and several reductive transformations are applied. The 250 word limit proved critical and challenging, in that it forced summarizers to carefully choose information, essentially not covering the whole set of information from the source documents.
- Syntactic compression and rewriting is the last line of summarization, when it is obvious that more compression is needed.

As related to the evaluation process, we noted that there exists an inherent tendency for evaluators to determine whether a human or a machine performed the summarization. There were cases where evaluators altered their grading, because they inferred that not all texts were from humans or not all were from machines. We had noted this phenomenon also in MultiLing 2011. There are several cases where the evaluator also tries to determine the strategy of the system and, when one understands the underlying strategy, this may bias the grade. It would be interesting to evaluate this bias in the future.

Some additional notes are related to problems with the organization of the effort:

- A distributed work environment that would help track the progress of individuals and assignment of new tasks without significant communication effort, would have been very helpful.
- The assignment script was really critical in facilitating the organization of the effort and we plan to make it publicly available to allow reuse.

Overall, the collection and generation of the corpus was a very challenging effort, both in terms of organization and individual questions arising. However, next steps can build upon the lessons learnt, if the effort is well documented and the documents are freely and openly shared.

4.4 Romanian language

At MultiLing 2013, Romanian was addressed as a language for the first time. Following the Call for Contributors launched by the MultiLing organizers and based on the experience in the QA @ CLEF[4] evaluation campaign (Peñas et al., 2012), we started the data collection process working with a group of ten MSc students in Computational Linguistics from our Faculty, later adding another MSc student to the working group. Below we provide some notes on the translation and generation of human summaries processes:

- The translation, including verification, of the 150 WikiNews text documents from English into Romanian, was performed in a distributed context, theoretically based on an architecture like the one described in (Alboaie et al., 2003). Each student received one topic (10 documents) to be translated, based on a set of guidelines. We devised guidelines to tackle any language-dependent problems that need special care, and they were improved after each solution received from the students and based also on their questions. The full guidelines are provided in the Appendix of this document.

  We started with the following workflow: student A receives 10 English documents to be translated and summarized and sends the results to the organizer; another student, B, receives the English documents and the Romanian translations (made by student A) and s/he verifies the translations and prepares another summary. Finally, another student, C, receives from the organizer the 10 Romanian documents and s/he prepares the third summary of a given topic.

  Since the task proved to be very time-consuming for the students, all the last five topics (the ones introduced this year) were given to one student and then the translations were verified by the organizer.

[4]See `http://celct.fbk.eu/ResPubliQA/index.php` for more information.

- The generation of human summaries was performed immediately after the translation. For each topic, the aim was to create a summary that covers all the major points of the topic (what is major was left to summarizer' s discretion), being a self-sufficient, clearly written text, providing no other information than what is included in the source documents. The students were given no specific recommendations regarding the type of summary they should produce, e.g. an abstract versus an extract (Mani and Maybury, 1999), but they were specifically instructed to understand the main aspects of summarization.

5 Conclusions and lessons learnt

The corpus generated throughout the MultiLing corpus preparation provides a benchmark dataset for multilingual summarization. It tries to captured interesting, representative events, covering a variety of well-known news events around the world. The recent corporate interest in summarization, in conjunction with the ever-present increase of information flow from the Web and information redundancy, show that having a scientifically plausible set of evaluation tools for systems can help bring useful summarization systems to a wide audience. MultiLing functions as a focus point for multilingual summarization research and this document described the methods used to create a commonly accepted multilingual, multi-document summarization corpus.

Concerning thoughts on the future work of MultiLing, there are some points that have been raised by Contributors that we reproduce in the following sentences:

- In the translation phase, it would be useful to have translators for different languages discuss directly about some difficult cases, such as some ambiguous words, phrases and sentences, especially when they are expressed in some language-specific way.

- It would be very interesting to exploit the potential of comparable corpora, and not only of the parallel ones, especially if we consider the multilingual setting of MultiLing 2013. This means that the data should be collected starting from a given topic and each language contributor should find 10 documents on that given topic in his/her language.

- Creating a collaborative platform for building and improving summarization corpora could significantly facilitate the corpus building process for future efforts.

We remind the reader that a second paper (Elhadad et al., 2013) addresses the problems and challenges faced in the remaining languages actively contributed to in MultiLing 2013 (Czech, Hebrew and Spanish), thus completing the lessons learnt from the MultiLing 2013 contribution effort. Extended technical reports recapitulating discussions and findings from the MultiLing Workshop will be available after the workshop at the MultiLing Community website[5], as an addenum to the proceedings.

Acknowledgments

MultiLing is a community effort and this community is what keeps it alive and interesting. We would like to thank Contributors for their organizational effort, which made MultiLing possible in so many languages and all volunteers, helpers and researchers that helped realize individual steps of the process. A more detailed reference of the contributor teams can be found in Appendix A.

The MultiLing 2013 organization has been partially supported by the NOMAD FP7 EU Project (cf. `http://www.nomad-project.eu`).

References

[Alboaie et al.2003] Lenuta Alboaie, Sabin C Buraga, and Sınica Alboaie. 2003. tuBiG–a layered infrastructure to provide support for grid functionalities. *Omega*, 2:3.

[Cahan2013] Adam Cahan. 2013. Yahoo! To Acquire Summly `http://yodel.yahoo.com/blogs/general/yahoo-acquire-summly-13171.html`, March 25th.

[Dang and Owczarzak2008] H. T. Dang and K. Owczarzak. 2008. Overview of the TAC 2008 update summarization task. In *TAC 2008 Workshop - Notebook papers and results*, pages 10–23, Maryland MD, USA, November.

[Dang and Owczarzak2009] Hoa Trang Dang and K. Owczarzak. 2009. Overview of the tac 2009 summarization track, Nov.

[Dang2005] H. T. Dang. 2005. Overview of DUC 2005. In *Proceedings of the Document Understanding Conf. Wksp. 2005 (DUC 2005) at the*

[5]See `http://multiling.iit.demokritos.gr/pages/view/1256/proceedings-addenum`)

Human Language Technology Conf./Conf. on Empirical Methods in Natural Language Processing (HLT/EMNLP 2005).

[Dang2006] H. T. Dang. 2006. Overview of DUC 2006. In *Proceedings of HLT-NAACL 2006.*

[Elhadad et al.2013] Michael Elhadad, Sabino Miranda-Jiménez, Josef Steinberger, and George Giannakopoulos. 2013. Multi-document multilingual summarization corpus preparation, part 2: Czech, hebrew and spanish. In *MultiLing 2013 Workshop in ACL 2013*, Sofia, Bulgaria, August.

[Giannakopoulos and Karkaletsis2011] George Giannakopoulos and Vangelis Karkaletsis. 2011. Autosummeng and memog in evaluating guided summaries. In *TAC 2011 Workshop*, Maryland MD, USA, November.

[Giannakopoulos and Karkaletsis2013] George Giannakopoulos and Vangelis Karkaletsis. 2013. Summary evaluation: Together we stand npower-ed. In *Computational Linguistics and Intelligent Text Processing*, pages 436–450. Springer.

[Giannakopoulos et al.2008] George Giannakopoulos, Vangelis Karkaletsis, George Vouros, and Panagiotis Stamatopoulos. 2008. Summarization system evaluation revisited: N-gram graphs. *ACM Trans. Speech Lang. Process.*, 5(3):1–39.

[Giannakopoulos et al.2011] G. Giannakopoulos, M. El-Haj, B. Favre, M. Litvak, J. Steinberger, and V. Varma. 2011. TAC 2011 MultiLing pilot overview. In *TAC 2011 Workshop*, Maryland MD, USA, November.

[Hovy et al.2005] E. Hovy, C. Y. Lin, L. Zhou, and J. Fukumoto. 2005. Basic elements.

[Lin2004] C. Y. Lin. 2004. Rouge: A package for automatic evaluation of summaries. *Proceedings of the Workshop on Text Summarization Branches Out (WAS 2004)*, pages 25–26.

[Louis and Nenkova2012] Annie Louis and Ani Nenkova. 2012. Automatically assessing machine summary content without a gold standard. *Computational Linguistics*, 39(2):267–300, Aug.

[Mani and Maybury1999] Inderjeet Mani and Mark T Maybury. 1999. *Advances in automatic text summarization.* the MIT Press.

[Peñas et al.2012] Anselmo Peñas, Eduard H. Hovy, Pamela Forner, Álvaro Rodrigo, Richard F. E. Sutcliffe, Caroline Sporleder, Corina Forascu, Yassine Benajiba, and Petya Osenova. 2012. Overview of qa4mre at clef 2012: Question answering for machine reading evaluation. In *CLEF (Online Working Notes/Labs/Workshop).*

[Saggion et al.2010] H. Saggion, J. M. Torres-Moreno, I. Cunha, and E. SanJuan. 2010. Multilingual summarization evaluation without human models. In *Proceedings of the 23rd International Conference on Computational Linguistics: Posters*, page 1059–1067.

[Shih2013] Gerry Shih. 2013. Sound Familiar? After Yahoo Buys Summly, Google Buys News Summarization App Wavii `http://www.huffingtonpost.com/2013/04/24/google-wavii_n_3143116.html`, April 23rd.

[Tufis et al.2004] Dan Tufis, Dan Cristea, and Sofia Stamou. 2004. Balkanet: Aims, methods, results and perspectives. a general overview. *Romanian Journal of Information science and technology*, 7(1-2):9–43.

Appendix A: Contributor teams

Arabic language team

Team members Mahmoud El-Haj (Lancaster University, UK); Ans Alghamdi, Maha Althobaiti (Essex University, UK); Ahmad Alharthi (King Saud University, Saudi Arabia)

Contact e-mail m.el-haj@lancaster.ac.uk

Chinese language team

Team members Lei Li, Wei Heng, Jia Yu, Yu Liu, Qian Li

Team affiliation Center for Intelligence Science and Technology (CIST), School of Computer Science,Beijing University of Posts and Telecommunications,

Postal Address P.O.Box 310, Beijing University of Posts and Telecommunications, Xitucheng Road 10, Haidian District, Beijing, China

Contact e-mail leili@bupt.edu.cn

English and Greek languages team

Team members Zoe Angelou, Argyro Mavridakis, Valentini Mellas, Efrosini Zacharopoulou, George Kiomourtzis, George Petasis, George Giannakopoulos

Team affiliation NCSR "Demokritos"

Postal Address Institute of Informatics and Telecommunications, Patriarchou Grigoriou and Neapoleos Str., Aghia Paraskevi Attikis, Athens, Greece

Contact e-mail ggianna@iit.demokritos.gr

Romanian language team

Team members Corina Forascu, Raluca Moiseanu; Ana Maria Timofciuc, Alexandra Cristea, Alexandrina Sbiera, Bogdan Puiu, and Tudor Popoiu; other contributors to the task were Monica Ancuţa, Romică Iarca, Claudiu Popa, and Cosmin Vlăduţu

Team affiliation UAIC, Romania

Contact e-mail corinfor@info.uaic.ro

Appendix B: Romanian guidelines

1. Translation equivalents belonging to the same part of speech should be used. The Romanian words should be as "closest" as possible to their English equivalents: If the English word has as equivalent a cognate in Romanian, this one should be used. The Romanian wordnet[6] (Tufis et al., 2004) should be used for problematic situations. If the English word doesn' t have a Romanian cognate, then the translator should not try to paraphrase it. Example: The English "sporadic" will be translated into 'sporadic' , even though the translator would be tempted to use instead 'izolat' or 'rar' . It is not recommended to give translations such as 'mai puţin' or 'mai rar' .

2. English words should not be omitted and words which are not in the original English text should not be added because of stylistic reasons. Example: "The Telegraph" will be not translated when it refers to the newspaper and, moreover, the translators will not introduce an explanation, like 'cotidianul The Telegraph' [English: The Telegraph newspaper].

3. The Romanian diacritics have to be used, in UTF-8 encoding.

4. The translators must preserve as much as possible the tenses of the English verbs. Any disagreement from the English tense is allowed for linguistic reasons only (Romanian specific constructions), and not for stylistic ones.

5. The translators will preserve the format of dates, times, numbers. For example, for the issuing date of an article being "March 25, 2010" , the Romanian translation will be ' 25 martie 2010' and NOT 'Martie, 25, 2010' OR '25 Martie, 2010' .

6. The format of the numbers should follow the Romanian convention with respect to the decimal separator, which is comma (,), and not the period (.), like in English-speaking countries.

7. The unclear or unsure situations encountered by the translators will be separately recorded in a file, indicating the provenance of the document, the ID used for the problematic sentence and the commentaries/suggestions.

[6]See http://www.racai.ro/wnbrowser/.

Multi-document multilingual summarization corpus preparation, Part 2: Czech, Hebrew and Spanish

Michael Elhadad
Ben-Gurion Univ.
in the Negev, Israel
elhadad@cs.bgu.ac.il

Sabino Miranda-Jiménez
Instituto Politécnico
Nacional, Mexico
sabino_m@hotmail.com

Josef Steinberger
Univ. of
West Bohemia,
Czech Republic
jstein@kiv.zcu.cz

George Giannakopoulos
NCSR Demokritos, Greece
SciFY NPC, Greece
ggianna@iit.demokritos.gr

Abstract

This document overviews the strategy, effort and aftermath of the MultiLing 2013 multilingual summarization data collection. We describe how the Data Contributors of MultiLing collected and generated a multilingual multi-document summarization corpus on 10 different languages: Arabic, Chinese, Czech, English, French, Greek, Hebrew, Hindi, Romanian and Spanish. We discuss the rationale behind the main decisions of the collection, the methodology used to generate the multilingual corpus, as well as challenges and problems faced per language. This paper overviews the work on Czech, Hebrew and Spanish languages.

1 Introduction

In this document we present the language-specific problems and challenges faced by Contributors during the corpus creation process. To facilitate the reader we repeat some information found in the first part of the overview (Li et al., 2013): the MultiLing tasks and the main steps of the corpus creation process.

2 The MultiLing tasks

There are two main tasks (and a single-document multilingual summarization pilot described in a separate paper) in MultiLing 2013:

Summarization Task This MultiLing task aims to evaluate the application of (partially or fully) language-independent summarization algorithms on a variety of languages. Each system participating in the task was called to provide summaries for a range of different languages, based on corresponding corpora. In the MultiLing Pilot of 2011 the languages used were 7, while this year systems were called to summarize texts in 10 different languages: Arabic, Chinese, Czech, English, French, Greek, Hebrew, Hindi, Romanian, Spanish. Participating systems were required to apply their methods to a minimum of two languages.

The task was aiming at the real problem of summarizing news topics, parts of which may be described or may happen in different moments in time. We consider, similarly to MultiLing 2011(Giannakopoulos et al., 2011) that news topics can be seen as *event sequences*:

Definition 1 *An event sequence is a set of atomic (self-sufficient) event descriptions, sequenced in time, that share main actors, location of occurence or some other important factor. Event sequences may refer to topics such as a natural disaster, a crime investigation, a set of negotiations focused on a single political issue, a sports event.*

The summarization task requires to generate a single, fluent, representative summary from a set of documents describing an event sequence. The language of the document set will be within the given range of 10 languages and all documents in a set share the same language. The output summary should be of the same language as its source documents. The output summary should be between 240 and 250 words.

Evaluation Task This task aims to examine how well automated systems can evaluate summaries from different languages. This task takes as input the summaries generated from automatic systems and humans in the Summarization Task. The output should be a grading of the summaries. Ideally, we would want the automatic evaluation to maximally correlate to human judgement.

The first task was aiming at the real problem of summarizing news topics, parts of which may be described or happen in different moments in time. The implications of including multiple aspects of the same event, as well as time relations at a varying level (from consequtive days to years), are still difficult to tackle in a summarization context. Furthermore, the requirement for multilingual applicability of the methods, further accentuates the difficulty of the task.

The second task, summarization evaluation has come to be a prominent research problem, based on the difficulty of the summary evaluation process. While commonly used methods build upon a few human summaries to be able to judge automatic summaries (e.g., (Lin, 2004; Hovy et al., 2005)), there also exist works on fully automatic evaluation of summaries, without human "model" summaries (Louis and Nenkova, 2012; Saggion et al., 2010). The Text Analysis Conference has a separate track, named AESOP (Dang and Owczarzak, 2009) aiming to test and evaluate different automatic evaluation methods of summarization systems.

Given the tasks, a corpus needed to be generated, that would be able to:

- provide input texts in different languages to summarization systems.

- provide model summaries in different languages as gold standard summaries, to also allow for automatic evaluation using model-dependent methods.

- provide human grades to automatic and human summaries in different languages, to support the testing of summary evaluation systems.

In the following section we show how these requirements were met in MultiLing 2013.

3 Corpus collection and generation

The overall process of creating the corpus of MultiLing 2013 was, similarly to MultiLing 2011, based on a community effort. The main processes consisting the generation of the corpus are as follows:

- Selection of a source corpus in a single language.

- Translation of the source corpus to different languages.

- Human summarization of corpus topics per language.

- Evaluation of human summaries, as well as of submitted system runs.

4 Language specific notes

In the following paragraphs we provide language-specific overviews related to the corpus contribution effort. The aim of these overviews is to provide a reusable pool of knowledge for future similar efforts.

In this document we elaborate on Czech, Hebrew, and Spanish languages. A second document (Elhadad et al., 2013) elaborates on the rest of the languages.

4.1 Czech language

The first part of the Czech subcorpus (10 topics) was created for the multilingual pilot task at TAC 2011. Five new topics were added for Multiling 2013. In total, 14 annotators participated in the Czech corpus creation.

The most time consuming part of the annotation work was the translation of the articles. The annotators were not professional translators and many topics required domain knowledge for correct translation. To be able to translate a person name, the translator needs to know its correct spelling in Czech, which is usually different from English. The gender also plays an important role in the translation, because a suffix 'ová' must be added to female surnames.

Translation of organisation names or person's functions within an organisation needs some domain knowledge as well. Complicated morphology and word order in Czech (more free but sometimes very different from English) makes the translation even more difficult.

For the creation of model summaries the annotator needed to analyse the topic well in order to decide what is important and what is redundant. Sometimes, it was very difficult, mainly in the case of topics which covered a long period (even 5 years) and which contained articles sharing very little information.

The main question of the evaluation part was how to evaluate a summary which contains a readable, continuous text — mainly the case of the

Group	SysID	Avg Perf
a	B	4.75
a	A	4.63
ab	C	4.61
b	D	4.21
b	E	4.10

Table 1: Czech: Tukey's HSD test groups for human summarizers

baseline system with ID6) — however not important information from the article cluster point of view.

An overview of the Overall Responsiveness and the corresponding average grades of the human summarizers can be seen in Table 1. We note that on average the human summaries are considered excellent (graded above 4 out of 5), but that there exist statistically significant differences between summarizers, essentially forming two distinct groups.

4.2 Hebrew language

This section describes the process of preparing the dataset for MultiLing 2013 in Hebrew: translation of source texts from English, and the summarization for the translated texts, by the Ben Gurion University Natural Language Processing team.

4.2.1 Translation Process

Four people participated in the translation and the summarization of the dataset of the 50 news articles: three graduate students, one a native English speaker with fluent Hebrew and the other two with Hebrew as a mother tongue and very good English skills. The process was supervised by a professional translator with a doctoral degree with experience in translation and scientific editing.

The average times to read an article was 2.5 minutes (std. dev 1.2min), the average translation time was 30 minutes (std. dev 15min), and the average proofing time was 18.5min (std. dev 10.5min).

4.2.2 Translation Methodology

We tested two translation methodologies by different translators. In some of the cases, translation was aided with Google Translate[1], while in other cases, translation was performed from scratch.

In the cases where texts were first translated using Google Translate, the translator reviewed the text and edited changes according to her judgment. Relying on the time that was reported for the proofreading of each translation, we could tell that texts that were translated using this method, required longer periods of proofreading (and sometimes more time was required to proofread than to translate). This is most likely because once the automatic translation was available, the human translator was biased by the automatic outcome, remaining anchored' to the given text with reduced criticism and creativity.

Translating the text manually, aided with online or offline dictionaries, Wikipedia and news site on the subject that was translated, showed better quality as analysis of time shows, where the ratio between the time needed to proofread was less than half.

In addition, we found, that in most cases the time that the translation took for the first texts of a given subject (for each article cluster), tends to be significantly longer than the subsequent articles in the same cluster. This reflects the 'learning phase' experienced by the translators who approached each cluster, getting to know the vocabulary of each subject.

4.2.3 Topic Clusters

The text collection includes five clusters of ten articles each. Some of the topics were very familiar to the Hebrew-speaking readers, and some subjects were less familiar or relevant. The Iranian Nuclear issue is very common in the local news and terminology is well known. Moreover, it was possible to track the articles from the news as they were published in Hebrew news websites at that time; this was important for the usage of actual and correct news-wise terminology. The hardest batch to translate was on the Paralympics championship, which had no publicity in Hebrew, and the terminology of winter sports is culturally foreign to native Hebrew speakers.

4.2.4 Special Issues in Hebrew

A couple of issues have surfaced during the translation and should be noted. Many words in Hebrew have a foreign transliterated usage and an original Hebrew word as well. For instance, the Latin word Atomic is very common in Hebrew and, therefore, it will be equally acceptable to use it in the Hebrew form, אטומי / 'atomi' but also the Hebrew word גרעיני ('gar' ini' / nuclear). Traditional Hebrew News Agencies have for many

[1] See http://translate.google.com/.

Summarizer	Reading time	Summarization
A	43 min	49 min
B	22 min	84 min
C	35 min	62 min

Table 2: Summarization process times (averaged)

years adopted an editorial line which strongly encourages using original Hebrew words whenever possible. In recent years, however, this approach is relaxed, and both registers are equally accepted. We have tried to use a 'common notion' in all texts using the way terms are written in Wikipedia as the voice of majority. In most cases, this meant using many transliterations.

Another issue in Hebrew concerns the orthography variations of plene vs. deficient spelling. Since Hebrew can be written with or without vocalization, words may be written with variations. For instance, the vocalized version of the word 'air' is אֲוִיר ('avir') while the non-vocalized version is אוויר ('avvir'). The rules of spelling related to these variations are complicated and are not common knowledge. Even educated people write words with high variability, and in many cases, usage is skewed by the rules embedded in the Microsoft Word editor. We did not make any specific effort to enforce standard spelling in the dataset.

4.2.5 Summarization Process

Each cluster of articles was summarized by three persons, and each summary was proof-read by the other summarizers. Most of the summarizers read the texts before summarization, while translating or proofreading them, and, therefore, the time that was required to read all texts was reduced.

The time spent reading and summarizing was extremely different for each of the three summarizers, reflecting widely different summarization strategies, as indicated in the Table 2 (average times over the 5 new clusters of MultiLing 2013):

The trend indicates that investing more time up front reading the clusters pays off later in summarization time.

The instructions did not explicitly recommend abstractive vs. extractive summarization. Two summarizers applied abstractive methods, one tended to use mostly extractive (C). The extractive method did not take markedly less time than the abstractive one. In the evaluation, the extractive summary was found markedly less fluent.

Group	SysID	Avg Perf
a	A	4.80
ab	B	4.40
b	C	4.13

Table 3: Hebrew: Tukey's HSD test groups for human summarizers

As the best technique to summarize efficiently, all summarizers found that ordering the texts by date of publication was the best way to conduct the summaries in the most fluent manner.

However, it was not completely a linear process, since it was often found that general information, which should be located at the beginning of the summary as background information, appeared in a later text. In such cases, summarizers changed their usual strategy and consciously moved information from a later text to the beginning of the summary. This was felt as a distinct deviation – as the dominant strategy was to keep track of the story told across the chronology of the cluster, and to only add new and important information to the summary that was collected so far.

The most difficult subject to summarize was the set on Paralympic winter sports championship which was a collection of anecdotal descriptions which were not necessarily a developing or a sequential story and had no natural coherence as a cluster.

4.2.6 Human evaluation

The results of human evaluation over the human summarizers are provided in Table 3. It is interesting to note that even between humans there exist two groups with statistically significant differences in their grades. On the other hand, the human grades are high enough to show high quality summaries (over 4 on a 5 point scale).

4.3 Spanish language

Thirty undergraduate students, from National Institute Polytechnic and Autonomous University of the State of Mexico, were involved in creating of Spanish corpus for MultiLing 2013.

The Spanish corpus built upon the Text Analysis Conference (TAC) MultiLing Corpus of 2011. The source documents were news from WikiNews website, in English language. The source corpus for translating consisted of 15 topics and 10 documents per topic. In the following paragraphs, we show the measured times for each stage and problems that people had to face during the generation of corpus that includes translation of documents, multi-document summarization, and evaluation of human (manual) summaries.

At the translation step, people had to translate sentence by sentence or paraphrase a sentence up to completing the whole document. When a document was translated, it was sent to another person to verify the quality of the translated document. The effort was measured by three different time measurements: reading time, translation time, and verification time.

The reading average at document level was 7.6 minutes (with a standard deviation of 3.4 minutes), the average translation of each document was 19.2 minutes (with a standard deviation of 7.8 minutes), and the average verification was 14.9 minutes (with a standard deviation of 7.7 minutes). The translation stage took 104.5 man-hours.

At summarization step, people had to read the whole set of translated documents (topic) and create a summary per each set of documents. The length of a summary is between 240 and 250 words. Three summaries were created for each topic. Also, reading time of the topic and time of writing the summary were measured.

The average reading of a set of documents was 31.6 minutes (with a standard deviation of 10.2 minutes), and the average time to generate a summary was 27.7 minutes (with a standard deviation of 6.5 minutes). This stage took 44.5 man-hours.

At evaluation step, people had to read the whole set of translated documents and assess its corresponding summary. The summary quality was evaluated. Three evaluations were done for each summary. The human judges assessed the overall responsiveness of the summary based on covering all important aspects of the document set, fluent and readable language. The human summary quality average was 3.8 (on a scale 1 to 5) (with a standard deviation of 0.81). The results are detailed in Table 4. It is interesting to note that all humans have no statistically significant differences in their grades. On the other hand, the human grades are not excellent on average (i.e. exceeding 4 out of 5) which shows that the evaluators considered human summaries non-optimal.

Group	SysID	Avg Perf
a	C	3.867
a	B	3.778
a	A	3.667

Table 4: Spanish: Tukey's HSD test groups for human summarizers

4.3.1 Problems during Generation of Spanish Corpus

During the translation step, translators had to face problems related to proper names, acronyms, abbreviations, and specific themes. For instance, the proper name "United States" can be depicted with different Spanish words such as "EE. UU." [2], "Estados Unidos", and "EUA" — all of them are valid words. Even though translators know all the correct translations, they decided to use the frequent terms in a context of news (the first two terms are frequently used).

In relation to acronyms, well-known acronyms were translated into equivalent well-known (or frequent) Spanish translations such as UN (United Nations) became into ONU (Organización de las Naciones Unidas), or they were kept in the source language, because they are frequently used in Spanish, for example, UNICEF, BBC, AP (the news agency, Associated Press), etc.

On the contrary, for not well-known acronyms of agencies, monitoring centers, etc., translators looked for the common translation of the proper name on Spanish news websites in order to create the acronym based on the name. Other translators chose to translate the proper name, but they kept the acronym from the source document beside the translated name. In cases where acronyms appeared alone, they kept the acronym from source language. It is a serious problem because a set of translated documents has a mix of acronyms.

Abbreviations were mainly faced with ranks such as lieutenant (Lt.), Colonel (Col.), etc. Translators used an equivalent rank in Spanish. For instance, lieutenant (Lt.) is translated into "teniente (Tte.)"; however, translators preferred to use the complete word rather than the abbreviation.

In case of specific topics, translators used Spanish websites related to the topic in order to know the particular vocabulary and to decide what (tech-

[2]The double E and double U indicate that the letter represents a plural: e.g. EE. may stand for Asuntos Exteriores (Foreign Affairs).

nical) words should be translated and how they should be expressed.

As regards at text summarization step, summarizers dealt with how to organize the summary because there were ten documents per topic, and all documents involved dates. Two strategies were employed to solve the problem: generating the summary according to representative dates, or starting the summary based on a particular date.

In the first case, summarizers took the chain of events and wrote the summary considering the dates of events. They gathered important events and put together under one date, typically, the latest date according to a part of the chain of events. They grouped all events in several dates; thus, the summary is a sequence of dates that gather events. However, the dates are chosen arbitrary according to the summarizers.

In the second case, summarizers started the summary based on a specific date, and continued writing the sequence of important events. The sequence of events represents the temporality starting from a specific point of time (usually, the first date in the set of documents). Finally, in most cases, evaluators think that human summaries meet the requirements of covering all important aspects of the document set, fluent and readable language.

5 Conclusions and lessons learnt

The findings from the languages presented in this paper appear to second the claims found in the rest of the languages (Li et al., 2013):

- Translation is a non-trivial process, often requiring expert know-how to be performed.

- The distribution of time in summarization can significantly vary among human summarizers: it essentially sketches different strategies of summarization. It would be interesting to follow different strategies and record their effectiveness in the multilingual setting, similarly to previous works on human-style summarization (Endres-Niggemeyer, 2000; Endres-Niggemeyer and Wansorra, 2004). Our find may be related to the (implied) effort of taking notes while reading, which can be a difficult cognitive process (Piolat et al., 2005).

- The time aspect is important when generating a summary. The exact use of time (a simple timeline? a grouping of events based on time?) is apparently arbitrary.

We remind the reader that extended technical reports recapitulating discussions and findings from the MultiLing Workshop will be available after the workshop at the MultiLing Community website[3], as an addenum to the proceedings.

What can definitely be derived from all the effort and discussion related to the gathering of summarization corpora is that it is a research challenge in itself. If the future we plan to broaden the scope of the MultiLing effort, integrating all the findings in tools that will support the whole process and allow quantifying the apparent problems in the different stages of corpus creation. We have also been considering to generate comparable corpora (e.g., see (Saggion and Szasz, 2012)) for future MultiLing efforts. We examine this course of action to avoid the significant overhead by the translation process required for parallel corpus generation. We should note here that so far we have been using parallel corpora to:

- allow for secondary studies, related to the human summarization effort in different languages. Having a parallel corpus is such cases can prove critical, in that it provides a common working base.

- be able to study topic-related or domain-related summarization difficulty across languages.

- highlight language-specific problems (such as ambiguity in word meaning, named entity representation across languages).

- fixes the setting in which methods can show their cross-language applicability. Examining significantly varying results in different languages over a parallel corpus offers some background on how to improve existing methods and may highlight the need for language-specific resources.

On the other hand, the significant organizational and implementaion effort required for the translation may turn the balance towards comparable corpora for future MultiLing endeavours.

[3]See http://multiling.iit.demokritos.gr/pages/view/1256/proceedings-addenum)

Acknowledgments

MultiLing is a community effort and this community is what keeps it alive and interesting. We would like to thank contributors for their organizational effort, which made MultiLing possible in so many languages and all volunteers, helpers and researchers that helped realize individual steps of the process. A more detailed reference of the contributor teams can be found in the Appendix.

The MultiLing 2013 organization has been partially supported by the NOMAD FP7 EU Project (cf. `http://www.nomad-project.eu`).

References

[Dang and Owczarzak2009] Hoa Trang Dang and K. Owczarzak. 2009. Overview of the tac 2009 summarization track, Nov.

[Elhadad et al.2013] Michael Elhadad, Sabino Miranda-Jiménez, Josef Steinberger, and George Giannakopoulos. 2013. Multi-document multilingual summarization corpus preparation, part 2: Czech, hebrew and spanish. In *MultiLing 2013 Workshop in ACL 2013*, Sofia, Bulgaria, August.

[Endres-Niggemeyer and Wansorra2004] Brigitte Endres-Niggemeyer and Elisabeth Wansorra. 2004. Making cognitive summarization agents work in a real-world domain. In *Proceedings of NLUCS Workshop*, pages 86–96. Citeseer.

[Endres-Niggemeyer2000] Brigitte Endres-Niggemeyer. 2000. Human-style WWW summarization. Technical report.

[Giannakopoulos et al.2011] G. Giannakopoulos, M. El-Haj, B. Favre, M. Litvak, J. Steinberger, and V. Varma. 2011. TAC 2011 MultiLing pilot overview. In *TAC 2011 Workshop*, Maryland MD, USA, November.

[Hovy et al.2005] E. Hovy, C. Y. Lin, L. Zhou, and J. Fukumoto. 2005. Basic elements.

[Li et al.2013] Lei Li, Corina Forascu, Mahmoud El-Haj, and George Giannakopoulos. 2013. Multi-document multilingual summarization corpus preparation, part 1: Arabic, english, greek, chinese, romanian. In *MultiLing 2013 Workshop in ACL 2013*, Sofia, Bulgaria, August.

[Lin2004] C. Y. Lin. 2004. Rouge: A package for automatic evaluation of summaries. *Proceedings of the Workshop on Text Summarization Branches Out (WAS 2004)*, pages 25–26.

[Louis and Nenkova2012] Annie Louis and Ani Nenkova. 2012. Automatically assessing machine summary content without a gold standard. *Computational Linguistics*, 39(2):267–300, Aug.

[Piolat et al.2005] Annie Piolat, Thierry Olive, and Ronald T Kellogg. 2005. Cognitive effort during note taking. *Applied Cognitive Psychology*, 19(3):291–312.

[Saggion and Szasz2012] Horacio Saggion and Sandra Szasz. 2012. The concisus corpus of event summaries. In *LREC*, pages 2031–2037.

[Saggion et al.2010] H. Saggion, J. M. Torres-Moreno, I. Cunha, and E. SanJuan. 2010. Multilingual summarization evaluation without human models. In *Proceedings of the 23rd International Conference on Computational Linguistics: Posters*, page 1059–1067.

Appendix: Contributor teams

Czech language team

Team members Brychcín Tomáš, Campr Michal, Fiala Dalibor, Habernal Ivan, Habernalová Anna, Ježek Karel, Konkol Michal, Konopík Miloslav, Krčmář Lubomír, Nejezchlebová Pavla, Pelechová Blanka, Ptáček Tomáš, Steinberger Josef, Zíma Martin.

Team affiliation University of West Bohemia, Czech Republic

Contact e-mail jstein@kiv.zcu.cz

Hebrew language team

Team members Tal Baumel, Raphael Cohen, Michael Elhadad, Sagit Fried, Avi Hayoun, Yael Netzer

Team affiliation Computer Science Dept. Ben-Gurion University in the Negev, Israel

Contact e-mail elhadad@cs.bgu.ac.il

Spanish language team

Team members Sabino Miranda-Jiménez, Grigori Sidorov, Alexander Gelbukh (Natural Language and Text Processing Laboratory, Center for Computing Research, National Institute Polytechnic, Mexico City, Mexico)

Obdulia Pichardo-Lagunas (Interdisciplinary Professional Unit on Engineering and Advanced Technologies (UPIITA), National Institute Polytechnic, Mexico City, Mexico)

Contact e-mail sabino_m@hotmail.com

Multi-document multilingual summarization and evaluation tracks in ACL 2013 MultiLing Workshop

George Giannakopoulos
NCSR Demokritos, Greece
SciFY NPC, Greece
ggianna@iit.demokritos.gr

Abstract

The MultiLing 2013 Workshop of ACL 2013 posed a multi-lingual, multi-document summarization task to the summarization community, aiming to quantify and measure the performance of multi-lingual, multi-document summarization systems across languages. The task was to create a 240–250 word summary from 10 news articles, describing a given topic. The texts of each topic were provided in 10 languages (Arabic, Chinese, Czech, English, French, Greek, Hebrew, Hindi, Romanian, Spanish) and each participant generated summaries for at least 2 languages. The evaluation of the summaries was performed using automatic and manual processes. The participating systems submitted over 15 runs, some providing summaries across all languages. An automatic evaluation task was also added to this year's set of tasks. The evaluation task meant to determine whether automatic measures of evaluation can function well in the multi-lingual domain. This paper provides a brief description related to the data of both tasks, the evaluation methodology, as well as an overview of participation and corresponding results.

1 Introduction

The MultiLing Pilot introduced in TAC 2011 was a combined community effort to present and promote multi-document summarization apporaches that are (fully or partly) language-neutral. This year, in the MultiLing 2013 Workshop of ACL 2013, the effort grew to include a total of 10 languages in a multi-lingual, multi-document summarization corpus: Arabic, Czech, English, French, Greek, Hebrew, Hindi from the old corpus, plus Chinese, Romanian and Spanish as new additions. Furthermore, the document set in existing languages was extended by 5 new topics. We also added a new track aiming to work on evaluation measures related to multi-document summarization, similarly to the AESOP task of the recent Text Analysis Conferences.

This document describes:

- the tasks and the data of the multi-document multilingual summarization track;
- the evaluation methodology of the participating systems (Section 2.3);
- the evaluation track of MultiLing (Section 3).
- The document is concluded (Section 4) with a summary and future steps related to this specific task.

The first track aims at the real problem of summarizing news topics, parts of which may be described or happen in different moments in time. The implications of including multiple aspects of the same event, as well as time relations at a varying level (from consequtive days to years), are still difficult to tackle in a summarization context. Furthermore, the requirement for multilingual applicability of the methods, further accentuates the difficulty of the task.

The second track, summarization evaluation, is related the corresponding, prominent research problem of how to automatically evaluate a summary. While commonly used methods build upon a few human summaries to be able to judge automatic summaries (e.g., (Lin, 2004; Hovy et al., 2005)), there also exist works on fully automatic evaluation of summaries, without human "model" summaries (Louis and Nenkova, 2012; Saggion et al., 2010). The Text Analysis Conference has a separate track, named AESOP (e.g. see (Dang and Owczarzak, 2009)) aiming to test and evaluate different automatic evaluation methods of summarization systems. We perform a similar task, but in a multilingual setting.

2 Multi-document multi-lingual summarization track

In the next paragraphs we describe the task, the corpus, the evaluation methodology and the results related to the summarization track of MultiLing 2013.

2.1 The summarization task

This MultiLing task aims to evaluate the application of (partially or fully) language-independent summarization algorithms on a variety of languages. Each system participating in the task was called to provide summaries for a range of different languages, based on corresponding corpora. In the MultiLing Pilot of 2011 the languages used were 7, while this year systems were called to summarize texts in 10 different languages: Arabic, Chinese, Czech, English, French, Greek, Hebrew, Hindi, Romanian, Spanish. Participating systems were required to apply their methods to a minimum of two languages.

The task was aiming at the real problem of summarizing news topics, parts of which may be described or may happen in different moments in time. We consider, similarly to MultiLing 2011 (Giannakopoulos et al., 2011) that news topics can be seen as *event sequences*:

Definition 1 *An event sequence is a set of atomic (self-sufficient) event descriptions, sequenced in time, that share main actors, location of occurence or some other important factor. Event sequences may refer to topics such as a natural disaster, a crime investigation, a set of negotiations focused on a single political issue, a sports event.*

The summarization task requires to generate a single, fluent, representative summary from a set of documents describing an event sequence. The language of the document set will be within the given range of 10 languages and all documents in a set share the same language. The output summary should be of the same language as its source documents. The output summary should be between 240 and 250 words.

2.2 Summarization Corpus

The summarization corpus is based on a gathered English corpus of 15 topics (10 of which were already available from MultiLing 2011), each containing 10 texts. Each topic contains at least one event sequence. The English corpus was then translated to all other languages (see also (Li et al., 2013; Elhadad et al., 2013)), trying to generate sentence-parallel translations.

The input documents generated are UTF8-encoded, plain text files. The whole set of translated documents together with the original English document set will be referred to as the *Source Document Set*. Given the creation process, the Source Document Set contains a total of 1350 texts (650 more than the corpus of the MultiLing 2011 Pilot): 7 languages (Arabic, Czech, English, Greek,) with 15 topics per language and 10 texts per topic for a total of 1050 texts; 3 languages (Chinese, French, Hindi) with 10 topics per language and 10 texts per topic for a total of 300 texts.

The non-Chinese texts had an average *word* length of approximately 350 words (and a standard deviation of 224 words). Since words in Chinese cannot be counted easily, the Chinese text length was based on the *byte* length of the corresponding files. Thus, Chinese texts had an average *byte* length of 1984 bytes (and a standard deviation of 1366 bytes). The ratio of average words in non-Chinese texts to average bytes in Chinese texts shows that on average one may (simplisticly) expect that 6 bytes of Chinese text are adequate to express one word from a European language.

We note that the measurement of Chinese text length in words proved a very difficult endeavour. In the future we plan to use specialized Chinese tokenizers, which have an adequately high performance that will allow measuring text and summary lengths in words more accurately.

2.3 Evaluation Methodology

The evaluation of results was perfromed both automatically and manually. The manual evaluation was based on the Overall Responsiveness (Dang and Owczarzak, 2008) of a text. For the manual evaluation the human evaluators were provided the following guidelines:

> Each summary is to be assigned an integer grade from 1 to 5, related to the overall responsiveness of the summary. We consider a text to be worth a 5, if

it appears to cover all the important aspects of the corresponding document set using fluent, readable language. A text should be assigned a 1, if it is either unreadable, nonsensical, or contains only trivial information from the document set. We consider the content and the quality of the language to be equally important in the grading.

The automatic evaluation was based on human, model summaries provided by fluent speakers of each corresponding language (native speakers in the general case). ROUGE variations (ROUGE-1, ROUGE-2, ROUGE-3, ROUGE-4) (Lin, 2004) and the AutoSummENG-MeMoG (Giannakopoulos et al., 2008; Giannakopoulos and Karkaletsis, 2011) and NPowER (Giannakopoulos and Karkaletsis, 2013) methods were used to automatically evaluate the summarization systems. Within this paper we provide results based on ROUGE-2 and MeMoG methods.

2.4 Participation and Overview of Results

This section provides a per-language overview of participation and of the evaluation results.

For an overview of participation information see Table 1. In the table, one can find the mapping between participant teams and IDs, as well as per language information. An asterisk in a cell indicates systems of co-organizers for the specific language. These systems had early access to the corpus for their language and, thus, had an advantage over others on that specific language.

Moreover, for the MultiLing pilot we created two systems, one acting as a global baseline (System ID6) and the other as a global topline (System ID61). These two systems are described briefly in the following paragraphs.

2.5 Baseline/Topline Systems

The two systems devised as pointers of a standard, simplistic approach and of an approach taking into account human summaries were implemented as follows.

The *global baseline system* — ID6 — represents the documents of a topic in vector space using a bag-of-words approach. Then it determines the centroid C of the document set in that space. Given the centroid, the system gets the text T that is most similar to the centroid (based on the cosine similarity) and uses it in the summary. If the text exceeds the summary word limit, then only a part of it is used to provide the summary. Otherwise, the whole text is added as summary text. If the summary is below the lower word limit, the process is repeated iteratively adding the next most similar document to the centroid.

The *global topline system* — ID61 — uses the (human) model summaries as a given (thus cheating). These documents are represented in the vector space similarly to the global baseline. Then, an algorithm produces random summaries by combining sentences from the original texts. The summaries are evaluated by their cosine similarity to the centroid of the model summaries.

We use the centroid score as a fitness measure in a genetic algorithm process. The genetic algorithm fitness function also penalizes summaries of out-of-limit length. Thus, what we do is that we search, using a genetic algorithm process, through the space of possible summaries, to produce one that mostly matches (an average representation of) the model summaries. Of course, using an intermediate, centroid representation, loses part of the information in the original text. Through this method we want to see how well we can create summaries by knowing a priori what (on average) must be included.

Unfortunately, the sentence splitting module of the topline, based on the Apache OpenNLP library[1] statistical sentence splitted failed due to a bug in our code. This resulted in an interesting phenomenon: the system would maximize similarity to the centroid, using fragments of sentences. This is actually an excellent way to examine what types of text can cheat n-gram based methods that they are good, while remaining just-not-good-enough from a human perspective. In the system performance analysis sections we will see that this expectation holds.

In the Tables of the following section we provide MeMoG and Overall Responsiveness (OR) statistics per system and language. We also provide information on statistically significant performance differences (based on Tukey HSD tests).

2.6 Language-specific Tables

The tables below illustrate the system performances per language. Each table contains three columns: 'Group', 'SysID' and 'Avg Perf'. The Group column indicates to which statistically

[1]See `http://opennlp.apache.org/`.

Participant	Run IDs	Arabic	Chinese	Czech	English	French	Greek	Hebrew	Hindi	Romanian	Spanish
Maryland	ID1, ID11, ID21	✓	✓	✓	✓	✓	✓	✓	✓	✓	✓
CIST	ID2	✓	✓*	✓	✓	✓	✓	✓	✓	✓	✓
Lancaster	ID3	✓*			✓						
WBU	ID4	✓	✓	✓*	✓	✓	✓	✓	✓	✓	✓
Shamoon	ID5, ID51	✓			✓			✓*			
Baseline	ID6	Centroid baseline for all languages									
Topline	ID61	Using model summaries for all languages									

Table 1: Participation per language. An asterisk indicates a contributor system, with early access to corpus data.

Group	SysID	Avg Perf
a	ID61	0.2488
ab	ID4	0.2235
abc	ID1	0.2190
abc	ID11	0.2054
abc	ID21	0.1875
abc	ID2	0.1587
abc	ID5	0.1520
bc	ID51	0.1450
bc	ID6	0.1376
c	ID3	0.1230

Table 2: Arabic: Tukey's HSD test MeMoG groups

equivalent groups of performance a system belongs. If two systems belong to the same group, they do not have statistically significant differences in their performance (95% confidence level of Tukey's HSD test). The SysID column indicates the system ID and the 'Avg Perf' column the average performance of the system in the given language. The caption of each table indicates what measure was used to grade performance. In the Overall Responsiveness (OR) tables we also provide the grades assigned to human summarizers. We note that for two of the languages — French, Hindi — there were no human evaluations this year, thus there are no OR tables for these languages. At the time of writing of this paper, there were also no evaluations for human summaries for the Hebrew and the Romanian languages. These data are planned to be included in an extended technical report, which will be made available after the workshop at the MultiLing Community website[2], as an addenum to the proceedings.

There are several notable findings in the tables:

- In several languages (e.g., Arabic, Spanish) there were systems (notable system ID4) that

[2]See `http://multiling.iit.demokritos.gr/pages/view/1256/proceedings-addenum`)

Group	SysID	Avg Perf
a	B	4.07
ab	C	3.93
ab	A	3.80
ab	ID6	3.71
ab	ID2	3.58
ab	ID3	3.58
ab	ID4	3.49
ab	ID1	3.47
abc	ID11	3.33
bcd	ID21	3.11
cde	ID51	2.78
de	ID5	2.71
e	ID61	2.49

Table 3: Arabic: Tukey's HSD test OR groups

Group	SysID	Avg Perf
a	ID4	0.1019
ab	ID61	0.0927
bc	ID2	0.0589
bc	ID1	0.0540
bc	ID11	0.0537
c	ID21	0.0256
c	ID6	0.0200

Table 4: Chinese: Tukey's HSD test MeMoG groups

Group	SysID	Avg Perf
a	B	4.47
a	C	4.30
a	A	4.03
b	ID2	3.40
c	ID4	2.43
c	ID61	2.33
c	ID21	2.13
c	ID11	2.13
c	ID1	2.07
d	ID6	1.07

Table 5: Chinese: Tukey's HSD test OR groups

Group	SysID	Avg Perf
a	ID61	0.2500
a	ID4	0.2312
ab	ID11	0.2139
ab	ID21	0.2120
ab	ID1	0.2026
b	ID2	0.1565
b	ID6	0.1489

Table 6: Czech: Tukey's HSD test MeMoG groups

Group	SysID	Avg Perf
a	B	4.75
ab	A	4.633
ab	C	4.613
ab	D	4.215
b	E	4.1
c	ID4	3.129
d	ID1	2.642
d	ID11	2.604
de	ID21	2.453
e	ID61	2.178
e	ID2	2.067
f	ID6	1.651

Table 7: Czech: Tukey's HSD test OR groups

Group	SysID	Avg Perf
a	ID4	0.2220
a	ID11	0.2129
a	ID61	0.2103
ab	ID1	0.2085
ab	ID21	0.1903
ab	ID6	0.1798
ab	ID2	0.1751
ab	ID5	0.1728
b	ID3	0.1590
b	ID51	0.1588

Table 8: English: Tukey's HSD test MeMoG groups

Group	SysID	Avg Perf
a	A	4.5
a	C	4.467
a	B	4.25
ab	D	4.167
ab	ID4	3.547
b	ID11	3.013
b	ID6	2.776
bc	ID21	2.639
bc	ID51	2.571
bc	ID61	2.388
bc	ID5	2.245
bc	ID1	2.244
bc	ID3	2.208
c	ID2	1.893

Table 9: English: Tukey's HSD test OR groups

Group	SysID	Avg Perf
a	ID4	0.2661
ab	ID61	0.2585
ab	ID1	0.2390
ab	ID11	0.2353
ab	ID21	0.2180
ab	ID6	0.1956
b	ID2	0.1844

Table 10: French: Tukey's HSD test MeMoG groups

Group	SysID	Avg Perf
a	ID61	0.2179
ab	ID11	0.1825
ab	ID1	0.1783
ab	ID21	0.1783
ab	ID4	0.1727
b	ID2	0.1521
b	ID6	0.1393

Table 11: Greek: Tukey's HSD test MeMoG groups

Group	SysID	Avg Perf
a	A	3.889
a	ID4	3.833
a	B	3.792
a	C	3.792
a	D	3.583
ab	ID11	2.878
ab	ID6	2.795
ab	ID1	2.762
ab	ID21	2.744
ab	ID61	2.717
b	ID2	2.389

Table 12: Greek: Tukey's HSD test OR groups

Group	SysID	Avg Perf
a	ID61	0.219
ab	ID11	0.1888
ab	ID4	0.1832
ab	ID21	0.1668
ab	ID51	0.1659
ab	ID1	0.1633
ab	ID5	0.1631
b	ID6	0.1411
b	ID2	0.1320

Table 13: Hebrew: Tukey's HSD test MeMoG groups

Group	SysID	Avg Perf
a	ID11	0.1490
a	ID4	0.1472
a	ID2	0.1421
a	ID21	0.1402
a	ID61	0.1401
a	ID1	0.1365
a	ID6	0.1208

Table 14: Hindi: Tukey's HSD test MeMoG groups

Group	SysID	Avg Perf
a	ID61	0.2308
a	ID4	0.2100
a	ID1	0.2096
a	ID21	0.1989
a	ID11	0.1959
a	ID6	0.1676
a	ID2	0.1629

Table 15: Romanian: Tukey's HSD test MeMoG groups

Group	SysID	Avg Perf
a	ID4	4.336
ab	ID6	4.033
bc	ID11	3.433
c	ID1	3.329
c	ID21	3.207
c	ID61	3.051
c	ID2	2.822

Table 16: Romanian: Tukey's HSD test OR groups

Group	SysID	Avg Perf
a	ID4	0.2516
a	ID61	0.2491
ab	ID11	0.2399
ab	ID1	0.2261
ab	ID21	0.2083
ab	ID2	0.2075
b	ID6	0.187

Table 17: Spanish: Tukey's HSD test MeMoG groups

Group	SysID	Avg Perf
a	C	3.867
a	ID4	3.844
a	B	3.778
ab	A	3.667
abc	ID6	3.444
bc	ID2	3.067
c	ID11	3.022
c	ID1	2.978
c	ID21	2.956
c	ID61	2.844

Table 18: Spanish: Tukey's HSD test OR groups

reached human level performance.

- The centroid baseline performed very well in several cases (e.g., Spanish, Arabic), while rather badly in others (e.g., Czech).
- The cheating topline system did indeed manage to reveal a blind-spot of automatic evaluation, achieving high MeMoG grades, while performing badly in terms of OR grade.

We note that detailed results related to the performances of the participants will be made available via the MultiLing website[3].

3 Automatic Evaluation track

In the next paragraphs we describe the task, the corpus and the evaluation methodology related to the automatic summary evaluation track of MultiLing 2013.

3.1 The Evaluation Task

This task aims to examine how well automated systems can evaluate summaries from different languages. This task takes as input the summaries generated from automatic systems and humans in the Summarization Task. The output should be a grading of the summaries. Ideally, we would want the automatic evaluation to maximally correlate to human judgement.

3.2 Evaluation Corpus

Based on the Source Document Set, a number of human summarizers and several automatic systems submitted summaries for the different topics in different languages. The human summaries were considered model summaries and were provided, together with the source texts and the automatic summaries, as input to summary evaluation systems. There were a total of 405 model summaries and 929 automatic summaries (one system did not submit summaries for all the topics). Each topic in each language was mapped to 3 model summaries.

The question posed in the multi-lingual context is whether an automatic measure is enough to provide a ranking of systems. In order to answer this question we used the ROUGE-2 score, as well as the "n-gram graph"-based methods (AutoSummENG, MeMoG, NPowER) to grade summaries. We used ROUGE-2 because it has been robust and highly used for several years in the DUC and TAC communities. There was only one additional participating measure for the evaluation track — namely the Coverage measure — in addition to the above methods.

In order to measure correlation we used Kendall's Tau, to see whether grading with the automatic or the manual grades would cause different rankings (and how different). The results of the correlation per language are indicated in Table 19. Unfortunately, the Hebrew evaluation data were not fully available at the time of writing and, thus, they could not be used. Please check the technical report tha twill be available after the completion of the Workshop for more information[4].

4 Summary and Future Directions

Overall, the MultiLing 2013 multi-document summarization and summary evaluation tasks aimed to provide a scientifically acceptable benchmark setting for summarization systems. Building upon previous community effort we managed to achieve two main aims of the MultiLing Pilot of 2011 (Giannakopoulos et al., 2011): we managed to increase the number of languages included to 10 and increase the number of topics per language.

We should also note that the addition of Chinese topics offered a fresh set of requirements, related to the differences of writing in this specific language from writing in the rest of the languages in the corpus: not even tokenization is easy to transfer to Chinese from other,e.g. European languages.

The main lessons learned from the multi-document and evaluation tracks were the following:

- multi-document summarization is an active domain of research.
- current systems seem to perform well-enough to provide more than basic, acceptable services to humans in a variety of languages. However, there still exist challenging languages.
- there are languages where systems achieved human-grade performance.
- automatic evaluation of summaries in different languages in far from an easy task. Much more effort must be put in this direction, to facilitate summarization research.

[3]See `http://multiling.iit.demokritos.gr`

[4]See `http://multiling.iit.demokritos.gr/pages/view/1256/proceedings-addenum)`

Language	R2 to OR	MeMoG to OR	Coverage to OR
Arabic	-0.11	0.00	-0.07
Chinese	**-0.38**	**0.46**	**0.41**
Czech	**0.38**	**0.30**	**0.26**
English	**0.22**	**0.24**	**0.26**
Greek	0.07	0.07	0.03
Romanian	**0.15**	**0.16**	**0.12**
Spanish	0.01	0.05	0.04
All languages	**0.12**	**0.18**	**0.14**

Table 19: Correlation (Kendall's Tau) Between Gradings. Note: statistically significant results, with p-value < 0.05, in **bold**.

The main steps we plan to take, based also on the future steps inherited from the MultiLing Pilot of 2011 are:

- to find the funds required for the evaluation process, in order to support the quality of the endeavour.
- to use the top performing evaluation system as the main evaluation measure in future MultiLing workshops.
- to create a piece of support software that will help implement and track all corpus generation processes.
- to study the possibility of breaking down the summarization process and asking systems to make individual components available as (web) services to other systems. This practice aims to allow combinations of different components into new methods.
- to check the possibility of using the corpus for cross-language summarization. We can either have the task of generating a summary in a different language than the source documents, or/and use multi-language source documents on a single topic to provide a summary in one target language.
- to start a track aiming to measure the effectiveness of multi-lingual summarization as a commercial service to all the world. This track would need a common interface, hiding the underlying mechanics from the user. The user, in turn, will be requested to judge a summary based on its extrinsic value. Much conversation needs to be conducted in order for this task to provide a meaningful comparison between systems. The aim of the track would be to illustrate the current applicability of multilingual multi-document summarization systems in a real-world task, aiming at non-expert users.

Overall, the MultiLing effort enjoys the contribution of a flourishing research community on multi-lingual summarization research. We need to continue building on this contribution, inviting and challenging more researchers to participate in the community. So far we have seen the MultiLing effort grow from a pilot to a workshop, encompassing more and more languages and research groups under a common aim: providing a commonly accepted benchmark setting for current and future multi-lingual summarization systems.

References

H. T. Dang and K. Owczarzak. 2008. Overview of the TAC 2008 update summarization task. In *TAC 2008 Workshop - Notebook papers and results*, pages 10–23, Maryland MD, USA, November.

Hoa Trang Dang and K. Owczarzak. 2009. Overview of the tac 2009 summarization track, Nov.

Michael Elhadad, Sabino Miranda-Jiménez, Josef Steinberger, and George Giannakopoulos. 2013. Multi-document multilingual summarization corpus preparation, part 2: Czech, hebrew and spanish. In *MultiLing 2013 Workshop in ACL 2013*, Sofia, Bulgaria, August.

George Giannakopoulos and Vangelis Karkaletsis. 2011. Autosummeng and memog in evaluating guided summaries. In *TAC 2011 Workshop*, Maryland MD, USA, November.

George Giannakopoulos and Vangelis Karkaletsis. 2013. Summary evaluation: Together we stand npower-ed. In *Computational Linguistics and Intelligent Text Processing*, pages 436–450. Springer.

George Giannakopoulos, Vangelis Karkaletsis, George Vouros, and Panagiotis Stamatopoulos. 2008. Summarization system evaluation revisited: N-gram graphs. *ACM Trans. Speech Lang. Process.*, 5(3):1–39.

G. Giannakopoulos, M. El-Haj, B. Favre, M. Litvak, J. Steinberger, and V. Varma. 2011. TAC 2011 MultiLing pilot overview. In *TAC 2011 Workshop*, Maryland MD, USA, November.

E. Hovy, C. Y. Lin, L. Zhou, and J. Fukumoto. 2005. Basic elements.

Lei Li, Corina Forascu, Mahmoud El-Haj, and George Giannakopoulos. 2013. Multi-document multilingual summarization corpus preparation, part 1: Arabic, english, greek, chinese, romanian. In *MultiLing 2013 Workshop in ACL 2013*, Sofia, Bulgaria, August.

C. Y. Lin. 2004. Rouge: A package for automatic evaluation of summaries. *Proceedings of the Workshop on Text Summarization Branches Out (WAS 2004)*, pages 25–26.

Annie Louis and Ani Nenkova. 2012. Automatically assessing machine summary content without a gold standard. *Computational Linguistics*, 39(2):267–300, Aug.

H. Saggion, J. M. Torres-Moreno, I. Cunha, and E. San-Juan. 2010. Multilingual summarization evaluation without human models. In *Proceedings of the 23rd International Conference on Computational Linguistics: Posters*, page 1059–1067.

ACL 2013 MultiLing Pilot Overview

Jeff Kubina
U.S. Department of Defense
9800 Savage Rd., Ft. Meade, MD 20755
jmkubin@tycho.ncsc.mil

John M. Conroy, Judith D. Schlesinger
IDA/Center for Computing Sciences
17100 Science Dr., Bowie, MD
conroy@super.org, drj1945@gmail.com

Abstract

The 2013 Association for Computational Linguistics MultiLing Pilot posed a task to measure the performance of multilingual, single-document, summarization systems using a dataset derived from many Wikipedias. The objective of the pilot was to assess automatic summarization of multilingual text documents outside the news domain and the potential of using Wikipedia articles for such research. This report describes the pilot task, the dataset, the methods used to evaluate the submitted summaries, and the overall performance of each participant's system.

1 Introduction

Document summarization is an active subject of research and development. The ACM Digital Library has about 806 reports on the subject published since 1993, with over half of them appearing in the last five years. While the impetus for much of this research is the annual Text Analysis Conference (TAC) workshop on document summarization, there is a growing demand in the consumer market for news summarization applications being met by tablet and smart-phone applications such as Clipped[1], Summoner[2], TLDR[3], and Yahoo News. Yahoo and Google even acquired two companies developing such applications, Summly (Stelter, 2013) and Wavii (Tsotsis, 2013) respectively, earlier this year. While summarization technology for news sources is coming to fruition, the performance of such technology on non-English documents outside the news domain has not been throughly assessed and may need further research. Since the datasets used by the TAC summarization workshops have predominately been English news articles, with some exceptions (Giannakopoulos et al., 2011), the objective of the 2013 ACL MultiLing Pilot was to assess the performance of automatic multilingual single-document summarization systems on non-English text outside the news domain and to determine the potential of using Wikipedia articles for such research.

This report starts with a description of the task and dataset, the methods used to evaluate the submitted summaries, the performance of each participating system, and concludes with an assessment of the pilot and potential future work.

[1]http://goo.gl/dFKD9
[2]http://goo.gl/0QFaZ
[3]http://goo.gl/qEgCs

2 Task and Dataset Description

The objective of each participant system of the pilot was simple: compute a summary for each document in at least two of the datasets languages. No restrictions were placed on the languages that could be chosen nor was any target summary size specified.

The dataset was derived from a corpus created in 2010 to measure the performance of the CLASSY (Conroy et al., 2009) summarization algorithm on non-English documents outside the news domain. At the time such a corpus did not exist so one was created from the Wikipedias. To date there are Wikipedias in 285 languages comprising over 75 million pages. Some of the Wikipedias maintain a list of *Feature Articles*, which are articles reviewed and voted upon by editors as the best that fulfill Wikipedia's requirements in accuracy, neutrality, completeness, and style. One such requirement is that the article have a lead section that should

> ... be able to stand alone as a concise overview. It should ... summarize the most important points ... [and] material in the lead should roughly reflect its im-

portance to the topic ...[4]

So the lead section of a featured article is an excellent summary of it, hence, the featured articles were used to create the corpus. In 2010 there were 41 Wikipedias with more than nine featured articles. The Perl module Text::Corpus::Summaries::Wikipedia[5] was developed to automatically create the corpus from the featured articles of those Wikipedias. The corpus is publicly available (Kubina, 2010) and the Perl module can be used to create an updated corpus.

The dataset for the pilot was created from a subset of the 2010 corpus. This was done to ensure that each language had 30 articles and that the size of each article's body text was sufficiently large. First, for each article the summary and body were compressed to approximate their information content size. For example, given a Chinese and English article with the same character length the Chinese article will usually contain more information than an English article and their compressed sizes will approximation their true information content. Next, if the compressed body size of an article was less than five times its compressed summary size, then the article was discarded. The factor of five was simply chosen to ensure the body of each article was sufficiently large relative to the summary size. For each language the median of the ratio of compressed body size to compressed summary size was computed and only the 30 articles closest to the median were included in the dataset. This filtering reduced the corpus from $12,819$ articles in 41 languages to the dataset containing $1,200$ articles in 40 languages. For each language in the dataset Table 1 contains the mean size of the articles, their bodies, and their summaries, in characters.

3 Evaluation Methods and Results

Four teams submitted the results of six summarization systems. The teams are denoted by AIS, LAN, MD, and MUS; the MD team submitted three systems. Throughout this report the systems are denoted by AIS, LAN, MD1, MD2, MD3, and MUS. Table 2 contains the list of languages submitted for each system and the mean size, in characters, of the summaries submitted.

For the evaluation a baseline summary was extracted from the each article in the dataset that is the prefix substring of the article's body text with the same length as the text in the lead section of the article. For the remainder of this report the lead section of an article is called the *human summary*. An oracle summary was also computed for each article by heuristically extracting sentences from its body text to maximize its ROUGE-2 score against the human summary until its size exceeded the human summary, upon which it was truncated.

Submitted summaries were automatically evaluated against the human summary of each article using ROUGE-1, ROUGE-2 (Lin, 2004) and MeMoG (Giannakopoulos et al., 2008). For ROUGE, the languages Chinese, Japanese, Korean, and Thai were tokenized into individual characters. For MeMoG the character n-gram size used for each language is listed in Table 3, which is the n-gram size that maximized the standard deviation divided by the mean of the n-gram frequency distribution of the language in the dataset. So the selected n-gram size maximizes the variability of the distribution values relative to their mean. A shorter n-gram size would inflate the MeMoG scores because of their inherent frequent co-occurrence and conversely a longer size would penalize MeMoG scores due to their infrequent co-occurrence.

Each scoring method was performed twice, first by truncating, if necessary, each system summary to the size of the human summary, which is called HSS-scoring. The second set of scores were computed by truncating *all* the summaries of an article, including the human summary, to the size of the shortest summary amongst the system and human summaries for the article, which is called SSS-scoring. For HSS-scoring the system summaries shorter that the human summary are penalized since ROUGE is *recall oriented*. Alternately, SSS-scoring gives preference to shorter system summaries that have their best content (extracted sentences) first.

The performance for HSS-scoring of the systems on the seven languages that at least two teams submitted summaries for are given in Figures 1, 2, and 3. Table 4 gives an overview of how often significant differences in each of the three automatic metrics was observed. In particular, the last row gives the fraction of times that an non-parametric analysis of variance (ANOVA) indicated that the

[4]http://en.wikipedia.org/wiki/Wikipedia:LEAD
[5]http://goo.gl/ySgOS

Table 1: Dataset Languages and Sizes

ISO	LANGUAGE	ARTICLE	BODY	SUMMARY
af	Afrikaans	24752 (10214)	23448 (10230)	1303 (196)
ar	Arabic	27845 (9490)	26354 (9530)	1491 (220)
bg	Bulgarian	23965 (9248)	22981 (9250)	984 (134)
ca	Catalan	30611 (15248)	29322 (15274)	1289 (140)
cs	Czech	26300 (10453)	24777 (10414)	1522 (190)
de	German	32023 (12522)	31160 (12530)	862 (53)
el	Greek	26072 (11113)	24937 (11096)	1134 (224)
en	English	26572 (9010)	24860 (9013)	1712 (114)
eo	Esperanto	22295 (10031)	21304 (10022)	990 (106)
es	Spanish	40467 (19563)	38726 (19533)	1740 (113)
eu	Basque	17886 (9845)	17231 (9821)	655 (91)
fa	Persian	15132 (7630)	14099 (7217)	1032 (517)
fi	Finnish	27379 (11783)	26353 (11805)	1025 (105)
fr	French	41578 (21952)	40186 (21959)	1392 (73)
he	Hebrew	18492 (8283)	17697 (8283)	794 (82)
hr	Croatian	21132 (11094)	20276 (11113)	855 (96)
hu	Hungarian	26256 (12161)	25175 (12139)	1081 (90)
id	Indonesian	18550 (9131)	17649 (9124)	901 (148)
it	Italian	39189 (19235)	38042 (19220)	1146 (80)
ja	Japanese	14352 (11890)	14131 (11895)	221 (38)
ka	Georgian	15282 (9570)	14558 (9551)	723 (124)
ko	Korean	17140 (7899)	16416 (7889)	724 (175)
ml	Malayalam	27329 (10645)	26158 (10639)	1170 (331)
ms	Malay	19346 (16577)	18436 (16348)	909 (411)
nl	Dutch	29575 (16346)	28580 (16363)	994 (89)
nn	Norwegian-Nynorsk	16107 (8056)	15384 (7917)	722 (297)
no	Norwegian-Bokmal	30225 (17652)	29218 (17594)	1006 (125)
pl	Polish	23028 (12853)	22067 (12861)	960 (66)
pt	Portuguese	30967 (17998)	29310 (18004)	1657 (110)
ro	Romanian	21921 (12812)	20782 (12773)	1139 (108)
ru	Russian	34069 (13792)	33134 (13771)	934 (70)
sh	Serbo-Croatian	21776 (21469)	21060 (21341)	716 (308)
sk	Slovak	21694 (10067)	20983 (10071)	711 (169)
sl	Slovenian	17900 (7222)	17077 (7194)	823 (135)
sr	Serbian	30239 (9812)	28927 (9764)	1312 (176)
sv	Swedish	23476 (10169)	22314 (10156)	1162 (99)
th	Thai	27041 (8312)	25425 (8291)	1616 (226)
tr	Turkish	32956 (16423)	31346 (16338)	1610 (257)
vi	Vietnamese	35376 (16099)	33857 (16050)	1518 (161)
zh	Chinese	10110 (4341)	9608 (4357)	501 (42)

Table 1: The table lists the languages in the dataset with the first column containing the ISO code for each the language, the second column the name of the language, and the remaining columns containing the mean size, in characters, and standard deviation, in parentheses, of the entire article, their bodies, and their summaries. For example, for English the mean size of the human summaries is 1,712 characters.

Table 2: Mean Summary Size For Submitted Languages of Systems

ISO	LANGUAGE	AIS	LAN	MD1	MD2	MD3	MUS	SUM
af	Afrikaans			966	953	967		1303
ar	Arabic		1461	876	858	874	2232	1491
bg	Bulgarian	1302		969	946	967		984
ca	Catalan			911	921	925		1289
cs	Czech			1061	1020	1062		1522
de	German	1492		1072	1037	1087		862
el	Greek	1367		989	979	991		1134
en	English	1262	1551	944	957	958	1197	1712
eo	Esperanto			947	933	956		990
es	Spanish			922	916	927		1740
eu	Basque			1154	1151	1167		655
fa	Persian			793	792	800		1032
fi	Finnish			1328	1284	1323		1025
fr	French			936	930	952		1392
he	Hebrew			871	867	876	1098	794
hr	Croatian			979	954	976		855
hu	Hungarian			1092	1064	1089		1081
id	Indonesian			1091	1085	1091		901
it	Italian			981	952	975		1146
ja	Japanese			546	564	563		221
ka	Georgian			1180	1195	1218		723
ko	Korean			663	638	656		724
ml	Malayalam			670	648	676		1170
ms	Malay			1089	1089	1098		909
nl	Dutch			994	974	1000		994
nn	Norwegian-Nynorsk			928	908	929		722
no	Norwegian-Bokmal			967	937	977		1006
pl	Polish			1086	1056	1083		960
pt	Portuguese			942	936	939		1657
ro	Romanian	1311		938	940	948		1139
ru	Russian			1095	1046	1078		934
sh	Serbo-Croatian			969	955	983		716
sk	Slovak			1026	997	1031		711
sl	Slovenian			967	949	981		823
sr	Serbian			990	954	979		1312
sv	Swedish			997	990	1006		1162
th	Thai			553	566	563		1616
tr	Turkish			1166	1132	1152		1610
vi	Vietnamese			696	684	691		1518
zh	Chinese			523	559	552		501

Table 2: The mean summary size, in characters, for each language submitted by each system including the mean of the human summaries in the last column named SUM.

Table 3: N-gram Size Per Language for MeMoG

Iso	Language	Size	Iso	Language	Size
af	Afrikaans	5	ka	Georgian	3
ar	Arabic	3	ko	Korean	1
bg	Bulgarian	4	ml	Malayalam	3
ca	Catalan	4	ms	Malay	4
cs	Czech	4	nl	Dutch	4
de	German	4	nn	Norwegian-Nynorsk	4
el	Greek	4	no	Norwegian-Bokmal	4
en	English	5	pl	Polish	4
eo	Esperanto	4	pt	Portuguese	4
es	Spanish	4	ro	Romanian	4
eu	Basque	4	ru	Russian	4
fa	Persian	4	sh	Serbo-Croatian	3
fi	Finnish	4	sk	Slovak	4
fr	French	4	sl	Slovenian	4
he	Hebrew	3	sr	Serbian	4
hr	Croatian	4	sv	Swedish	5
hu	Hungarian	4	th	Thai	3
id	Indonesian	5	tr	Turkish	5
it	Italian	5	vi	Vietnamese	5
ja	Japanese	1	zh	Chinese	1

Table 3: The table lists the n-gram size used for each language when evaluating summaries using MeMoG, which is the n-gram size that maximized the standard deviation divided by the mean of the n-gram frequency distribution of the language in the dataset.

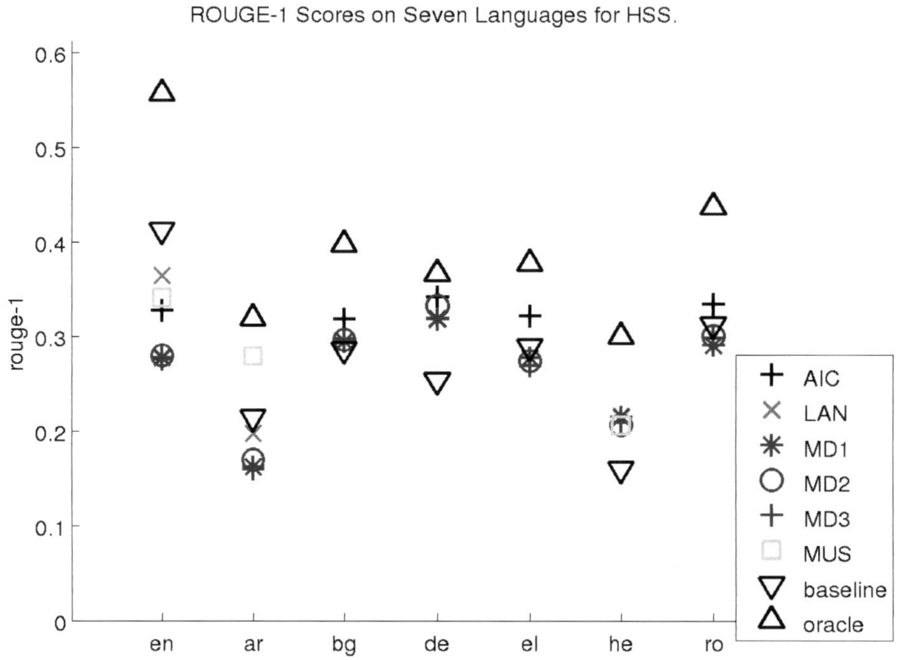

Figure 1: ROUGE-1 scores for HSS.

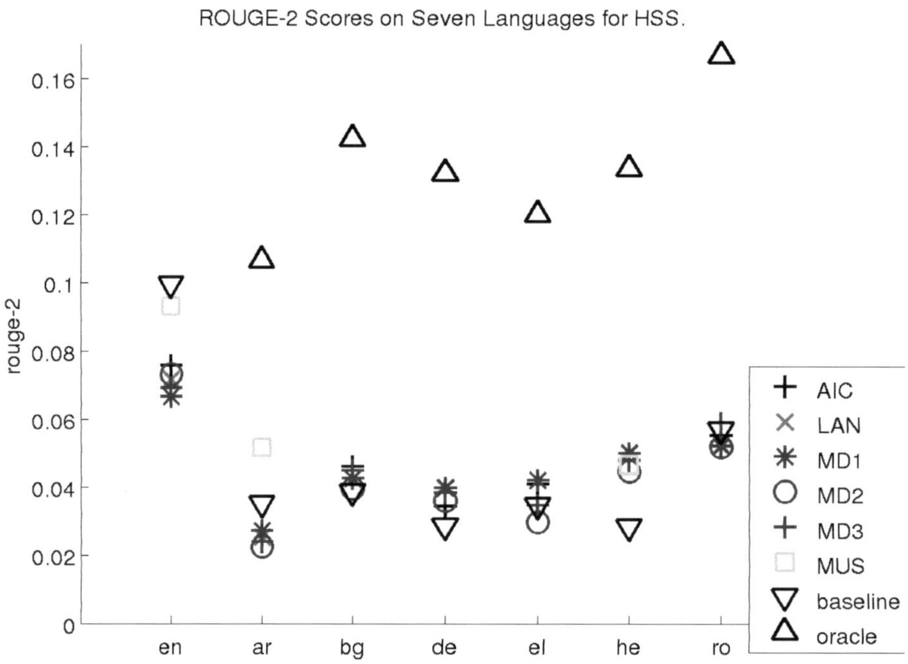

Figure 2: ROUGE-2 scores for HSS.

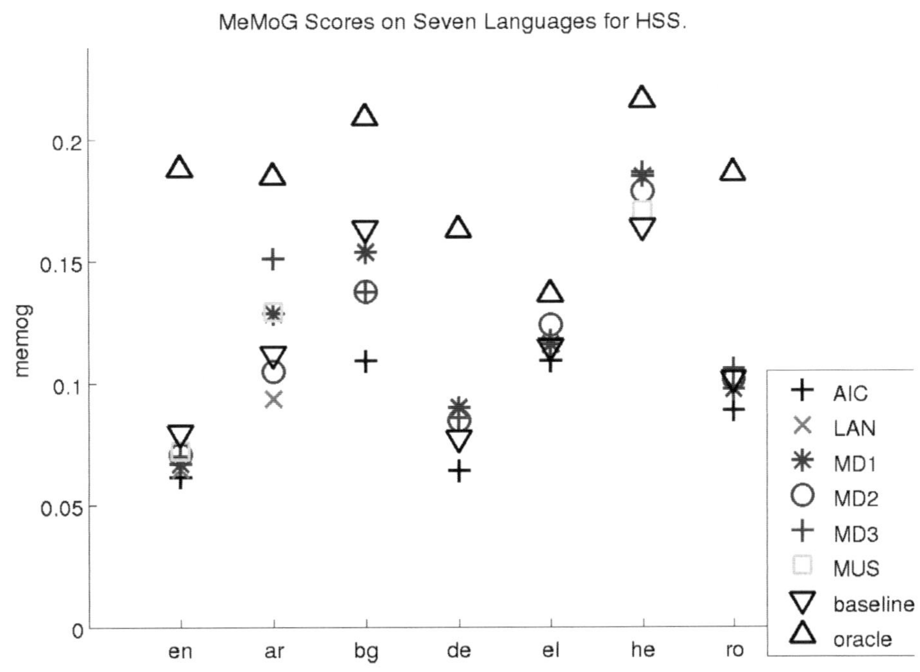

Figure 3: MeMoG scores for HSS.

Table 4: Fraction of time a system beat the baseline for HSS.

System	ROUGE-1	ROUGE-2	MeMoG
AIC	2/5	0/5	0/5
LAN	0/2	0/2	0/2
MD1	15/40	4/40	2/39
MD2	16/40	4/40	0/39
MD3	15/40	4/40	0/39
MUS	2/3	1/3	0/3
ANOVA	28/40	13/40	5/39

Table 4: The table gives the fraction of languages each system significantly outperform the baseline. The last line gives the number of times an ANOVA rejected the null hypothesis, indicating significance.

medians of the system scores were not the same, using a rejection threshold of 0.05. Also, the fraction of time that each system significantly outperformed the lead baseline is also recorded. A paired Wilcoxon test was invoked whenever the ANOVA indicated a significant difference was present, with a threshold of 0.05.

Lastly, each systems performance for SSS-scoring is provided in Figures 4, 5, and 6. Surprisingly, the results change little. Lastly Table 5 contains the number of times that each system beat the baseline summary with a 95% confidence measured as a result of the non-parametric ANOVA and the Wilcoxon paired sign rank test. The results show that the number of significant differences go down for ROUGE scores and up for MeMoG.

4 Summary

Overall, the authors believe the pilot was successful in that it exposed researchers to the potential for using Wikipedia articles for summarization research and demonstrated that generating summaries for the genre of Wikipedia articles is a more challenging task than newswire documents. Notably, no system outperformed the baseline for English! In hindsight this is not too surprising since news articles have a prose style[6] significantly different from Wikipedia articles[7]. Wikipedia articles are written as expositions having a topical flow that can vary significantly between sections but news articles are written in a style[8] that addresses the most important information first—the

[6] http://en.wikipedia.org/wiki/News_style
[7] http://en.wikipedia.org/wiki/MOS:
[8] http://en.wikipedia.org/wiki/Inverted_pyramid

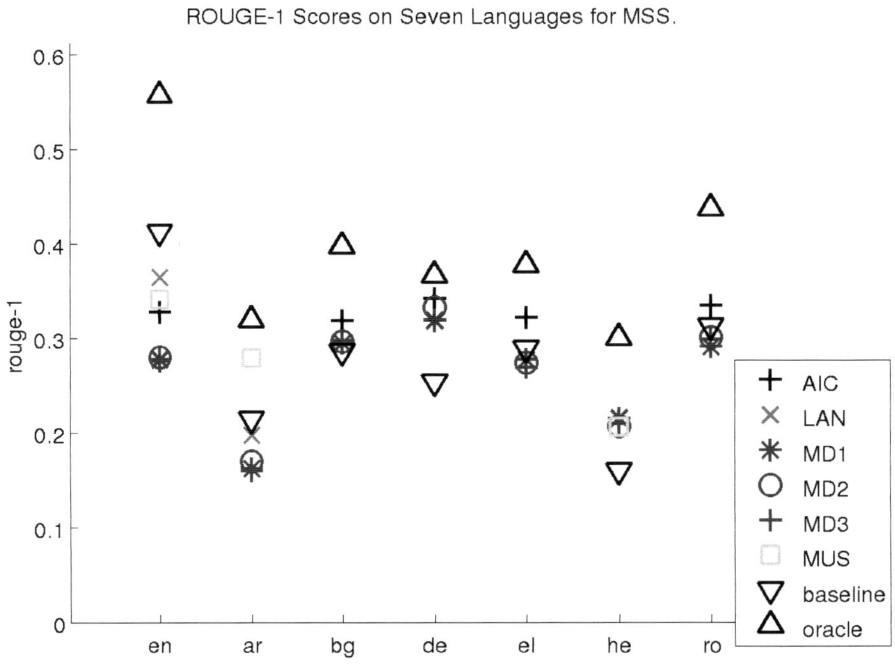

Figure 4: ROUGE-1 scores for SSS.

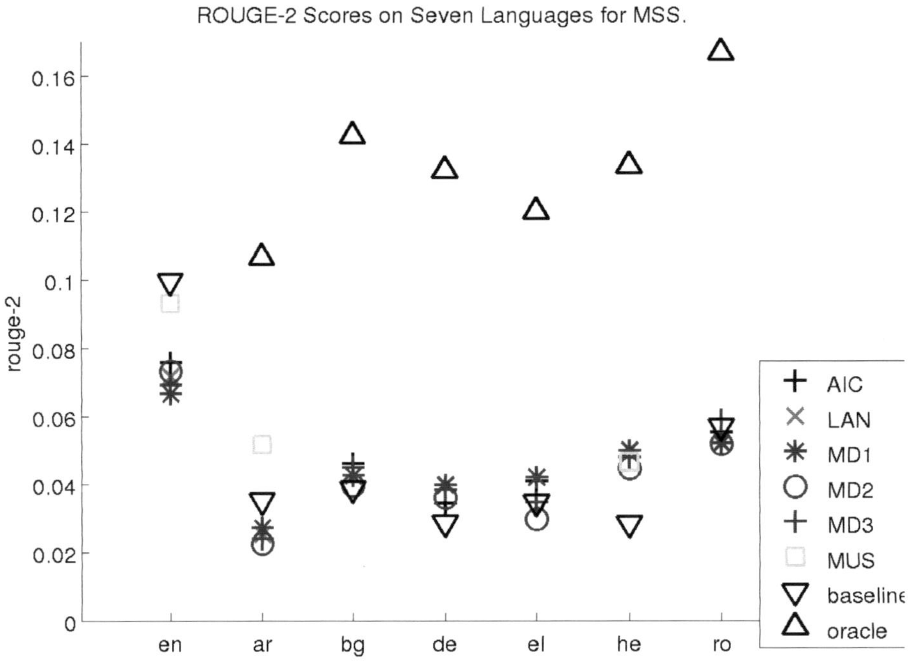

Figure 5: ROUGE-2 scores for SSS.

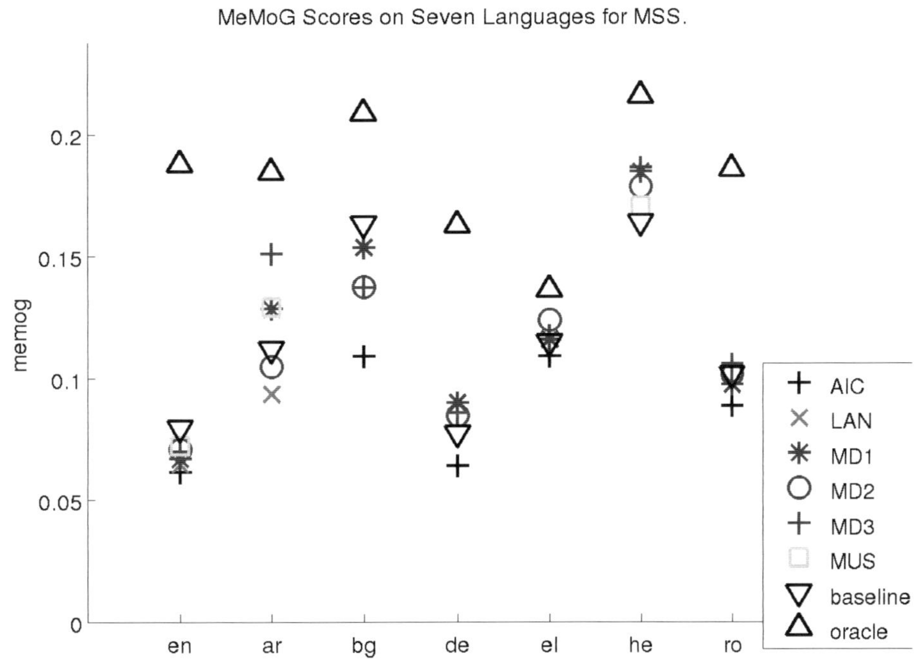

Figure 6: MeMoG scores for SSS.

Table 5: Fraction of the time a system beat the lead baseline for SSS.

System	ROUGE-1	ROUGE-2	MeMoG
AIC	0/5	0/5	0/5
LAN	0/2	0/2	0/2
MD1	8/40	2/40	6/39
MD2	10/40	2/40	2/39
MD3	7/40	2/40	4/39
MUS	0/3	0/3	0/3
ANOVA	11/40	5/40	7/39

Table 5: The table gives the fraction of languages that each system significantly outperform the baseline on. The last line contains the number of times an ANOVA rejected the null hypothesis, indicating significance.

who, what, when, where and why—with the subsequent text providing more details. Hence news articles have a more even topical flow. The authors hope these results stimulate research and development of summarization algorithms outside the news domain.

As for the metrics, ROUGE-1 observed the most significant differences among the systems and MeMoG observed the least as measured by a non-parametric ANOVA. However, a human evaluation of the summaries generated would be needed to detemine which of the automatic metrics is best at predicting significant differences among systems for such data.

References

John M. Conroy, Judith D. Schlesinger, and Dianne P. O'leary. 2009. Classy 2009: summarization and metrics. In *Proceedings of the text analysis conference (TAC)*.

George Giannakopoulos, Vangelis Karkaletsis, George Vouros, and Panagiotis Stamatopoulos. 2008. Summarization system evaluation revisited: N-gram graphs. *ACM Trans. Speech Lang. Process.*, 5(3):5:1–5:39, October.

George Giannakopoulos, Mahmoud El-Haj, Benoît Favre, Marina Litvak, Josef Steinberger, and Vasudeva Varma. 2011. Tac 2011 multiling pilot overview.

Jeff Kubina. 2010. Wikipedia featured article corpus. http://goo.gl/AmMGN. [Online; accessed 30-May-2013].

Chin-Yew Lin. 2004. Rouge: A package for automatic evaluation of summaries. In *Text Summarization Branches Out: Proceedings of the ACL-04 Workshop*, pages 74–81.

Brian Stelter. 2013. He has millions and a new job at yahoo. soon, he'll be 18. *New York Times*.

Alexia Tsotsis. 2013. Google buys wavii for north of $30 million. *TechCrunch*.

CIST System Report for ACL MultiLing 2013

-- Track 1: Multilingual Multi-document Summarization

Lei Li, Wei Heng, Jia Yu, Yu Liu, Shuhong Wan
Center for Intelligence Science and Technology (CIST),
School of Computer Science and Technology,
Beijing University of Posts and Telecommunications (BUPT), China
leili@bupt.edu.cn

Abstract

This report provides a description of the methods applied in CIST system participating ACL MultiLing 2013. Summarization is based on sentence extraction. hLDA topic model is adopted for multilingual multi-document modeling. Various features are combined to evaluate and extract candidate summary sentences.

1 Introduction

CIST system has participated Track 1: Multilingual Multi-document Summarization in ACL MultiLing 2013 workshop. It could deal with all ten languages: Arabic, Chinese, Czech, English, French, Greek, Hebrew, Hindi, Romanian and Spanish. It summarizes every topic containing 10 texts and generates a summary in plain text, UTF8 encoding, less than 250 words.

2 System Design

There have been many researches about multi-document summarization, (Wan et al., 2006; He et al., 2008; Flore et al., 2008; Bellemare et al., 2008; Conroy and Schlesinger, 2008; Zheng and Takenobu, 2009; Louis and Nenkova, 2009; Long et al., 2009; Lin and Chen, 2009; Gong et al., 2010; Darling, 2010; Kumar et al., 2010; Genest and Lapalme, 2010; Jin et al., 2010; Kennedy et al., 2010; Zhang et al., 2011), but less about multilingual multi-document summarization (Leuski et al., 2003; Liu et al., 2011; Conroy et al., 2011; Hmida and Favre, 2011; Das and Srihari, 2011; Steinberger et al., 2011; Saggion, 2011; El-Haj et al., 2011).

This system must be applicable for unlimited topics, we couldn't use topic knowledge. Different topic has different language styles, so we use sentence as the processing unit and summarization method based on sentence extraction. It must also be available for different languages, we couldn't use much specific knowledge for all languages except one or two we understand. We refer to a statistical method, hLDA (hierarchical Latent Dirichlet Allocation (LDA)).

LDA has been widely applied. (Arora and Balaraman, 2008; Krestel et al., 2009). Some improvements have been made. (Griffiths et al., 2005; Blei and Lafferty, 2006; Wang and Blei, 2009). One is to relax its assumption that topic number is known and fixed. Teh et al. (2006) provided an elegant solution. Blei et al. (2010) extended it to exploit the hierarchical tree structure of topics, hDLA, which is unsupervised method in which topic number could grow with the data set automatically. There's no relations between topics in LDA (Blei, 2003), but hLDA could organize topics into a hierarchy, in which higher level topics are more abstractive. This could achieve a deeper semantic model similar with human mind and is especially helpful for summarization. Celikyilmaz (2010) provided a multi-document summarization method based on hLDA with competitive results. However, it has the disadvantage of relying on ideal summaries. To avoid this, the innovation of our work is completely dependent on data and hierarchy to extract candidate summary sentences.

Figure 1 and 2 show the framework for ten languages. Since Chinese Hanzi is different from other languages, we treat it with special processing. But the main modules are the same. The kernel one is constructing an hLDA model[1]. It's language independent.

[1] http://www.cs.princeton.edu/~blei/topicmodeling.html

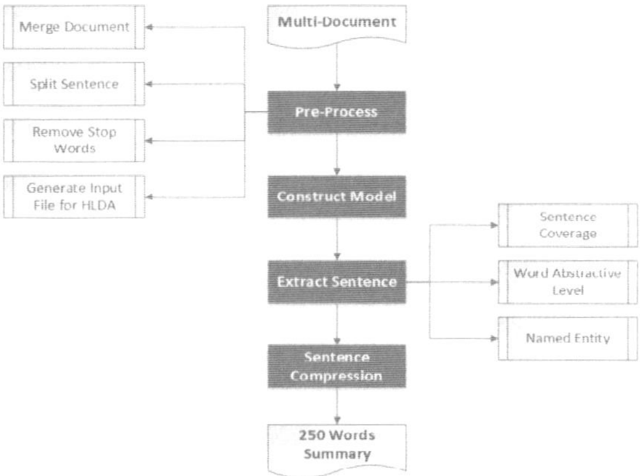

Figure 1: framework for nine languages (no Chinese)

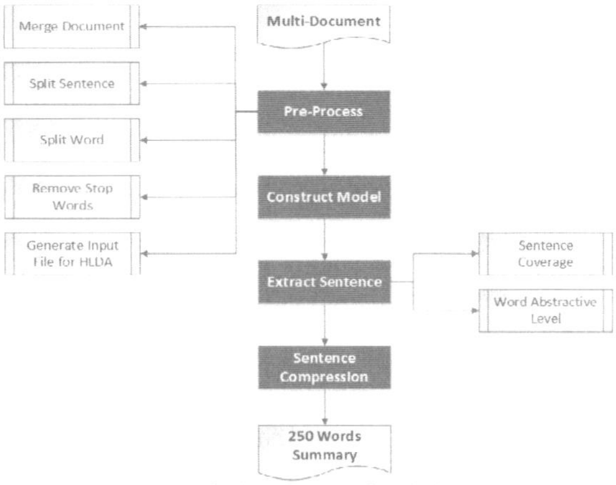

Figure 2: framework for Chinese

3 Text Pre-processing

There are some unified pre-processing steps for all languages and a special step for Chinese.

3.1 Merging Documents

We treat multi-document together, so we firstly combine them into a big text. As to Chinese, we combine and delete empty lines. As to other nine languages, we do this when we split sentences.

3.2 Splitting Sentences

We split sentences to get the processing unit. There are two lines of title and date ending with no punctuation mark. We add a full stop ourselves to avoid them being connected with the first sentence. For Chinese, we split sentences according to ending punctuation marks, while for other nine languages, the full stop "." could have other functions. We adopt machine learning method[2]. After some experiments, we choose Support Vector Machine model for English and French, Naïve Bayes model for other 7 languages.

[2] https://code.google.com/p/splitta/

3.3 Removing Stop Words

We add ICTCLAS[3] word segmentation to Chinese to make all languages have the same word separator. Then we could obtain words easily, among which are some stop words. We construct stop lists. For English and Chinese, the stop list contains punctuation marks and some functional words, while for other languages, it contains punctuation marks, which could unified the whole process easily although generally we do not treat punctuation marks as words. At the same time, all capitalized characters are changed to lower case.

3.4 Generating Input File for hLDA

We build a dictionary for remaining words, which are sorted according to frequency. The more frequent words are located before the less frequent ones. This is a mapping from word to a number varying from 1 to dictionary size. Finally we generate an input file for hLDA, in which each line represents a sentence, in the following form:

[number of words in the sentence] [wordNumberA]:[local frequencyA] [wordNumberB]:[local frequencyB]...

Figure 3 shows an example. As we can see that now it's language independent.

```
5 1:1 6:1 3:1 355:1 205:1
2 188:1 518:1
16 44:1 16:1 172:1 13:1 5:1 1:1 2:1 6:1 207:1 197:1 768:1 794:1 355:1
39:1 3:1 231:1
8 6:1 65:1 949:1 227:1 333:1 19:1 20:1 247:1
18 691:1 162:1 41:1 433:1 493:1 0:1 395:1 8:1 11:1 15:1 32:1 4:1 646:1
183:1 726:1 541:1 382:1 27:1
```

Figure 3: hLDA input file

4 hLDA Topic Modeling

Given a collection of sentences in the input file, we wish to discover common usage patterns or topics and organize them into a hierarchy. Each node is associated with a topic, which is a distribution across words. A sentence is generated by choosing a path from the root to a leaf, repeatedly sampling topics along that path, and sampling the words from the selected topics. Sentences sharing the same path should be similar to each other because they share the same sub-topics. All sentences share the topic distribution associated with the root node.

As to this system, we set hierarchy depth to 3, because we have found out in former experiments that 2 is too simple, and 4 or bigger is too complex for the unit of sentence.

[3] http://www.nlpir.org/download/ICTCLAS2012-SDK-0101.rar

4.1 Hierarchy Evaluation

In order to make sure that a hierarchy is good, we need to evaluate its performance. The best method is human reading, but it's too laborious to browse all topics and all languages. In fact, we could not understand all ten languages at all. So we build another simpler and faster evaluation method based on numbers. According to former empirical analysis, if a hierarchy has more than 4 paths and the sentence numbers for all paths appear in balanced order from bigger to smaller, and the sentences in bigger paths could occupy 70-85% in all sentences, then we could possibly infer that this hierarchy is good.

4.2 Parameter Setting

When facing a new corpus, we could hardly set the parameters automatically either by human or machine. There is a choice of sampling. We tried it for all languages with 100000 iterations. But the results are poor, even in the worst case each sentence is set to a single path. Thus we give up sampling and try to set the parameters by human.

We begin with Chinese because it seems to be the most difficult case. We randomly choose two topics for original testing and set some parameters according to former experience. Then we evaluate the result using method in 4.1. If it's not good, we go on to adjust the settings until we obtain a satisfactory result. The satisfied settings are then used originally for the whole corpus. Table 1 shows the details.

Parameter	Setting
ETA	1.2 0.5 0.05
GAM	1.0 1.0
GEM_MEAN	0.5
GEM_SCALE	100
SCALING_SHAPE	1.0
SCALING_SCALING	0.5
SAMPLE_ETA	0
SAMPLE_GAM	0

Table 1: Original parameter settings

Language	Topic
English	M006
Hebrew	M001 M006
Romanian	M002
Spanish	M003
Chinese	M004 M006

Table 2: original bad result

After running the whole corpus, we evaluate the results again. We found out that for most cases, the hierarchy is good, but there are some cases not so good, as shown in Table 2. So one set of parameter settings could not deal with all languages and topics successfully. The reason may be that different language and different topic must have different inherent features.

4.3 Parameter Adjustment

We analyze the bad results and try to adjust the settings. For instance, in English M006, there are only two paths indicating that the tree is too clustered. Parameter ETA should be reduced to separate more sub-topics. But too small ETA may lead to hLDA failure without level assignment result in limited iterations. So we also adjust GEM to get closer to the prior explanation of corpus. In some case, the numbers are assigned too much to the former big paths, then we should adjust SCALING parameters to separate some numbers to the smaller paths. For the bad cases in Table 2, we finally use the settings in Table 3.

Parameter	Setting
ETA	5.2 0.005 0.0005
GAM	1.0 1.0
GEM_MEAN	0.35
GEM_SCALE	100
SCALING_SHAPE	2.0
SCALING_SCALING	1.0
SAMPLE_ETA	0
SAMPLE_GAM	0

Table 3: Adjusted parameter settings

Figure 4 shows an example of the modeling result of M004 in English.

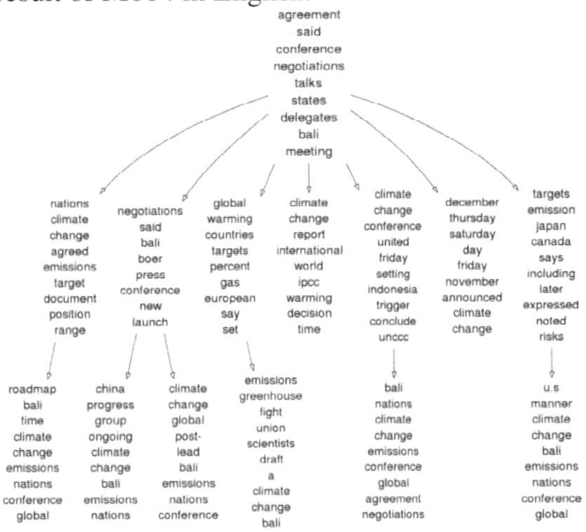

Figure 4: hLDA result example

5 Summary Generation

5.1 Sentence Evaluation

In the hLDA result, sentences are clustered into sub-topics in a hierarchical tree. A sub-topic is more important if it contains more sentences. Trivial sub-topics containing only one or two sentences could be neglected. Final summary should cover those most important sub-topics with their most representative sentences. We evaluate the sentence importance in a sub-topic considering three features.

1) Sentence coverage, which means that how much a sentence could contain words appearing in more sentences for a sub-topic. We consider sentence coverage of each word in one sentence. The sentence weight is calculated as eq.(1).

$$S_{tf} = \frac{\sum_{i=1}^{|s|} \frac{num_s(w_i)}{n}}{|s|} \quad (1)$$

Where w_i is the i_{th} word in sentence s, $num_s(w_i)$ is the number of sentences that w_i covers, | s | is the number of words in the sentence, and n is the total number of all sentences.

2) Word Abstractive level. hLDA constructs a hierarchy by positioning all sentences on a three-level tree. Level 0 is the most abstractive one, level 2 is the most specific one, and level 1 is between them. We evaluate the sentence abstractive feature as eq.(2).

$$S_l = a * \frac{num(W_0)}{|S|} + b * \frac{num(W_1)}{|S|} + c * \frac{num(W_2)}{|S|} \quad (2)$$

Where $num(W_0)$, $num(W_1)$, $num(W_2)$ are numbers of level 0, 1 and 2 words respectively in the sentence. There are three parameters: a, b and c, which are used to control the weights for words in different levels. Although we hope the summary to be as abstractive as possible, there is really some specific information we also want. For instance, earthquake news needs specific information about death toll and money lost.

3) Named entity. We consider the number of named entities in one sentence. This time we only have time to use Stanford's named entity recognition toolkit[4], which could identify English person, address and institutional names. If one sentence contains more entities, then it has a high priority to be chosen as candidate summary sentence. Let S_n be the number of named entity categories in one sentence. For example, if one sentence has only person names, then S_n is 1; else if it also has address information, then S_n is 2; else if it contains all three categories, then S_n is 3.

At last, we calculate sentence score S as eq. (3, 4), where d, e and f are feature weights:

English: $S = d * S_{tf} + e * S_l + f * S_n$ (3)

Others: $S = d * S_{tf} + e * S_l$ (4)

After experiments, we set {a, b, c, d, e, f} to {0.3, 1, 0.3, 2, 1, 0.05} for English, {a, b, c, d, e} to {1, 0.75, 0.25, 2, 1} for Chinese without M004 and M006, and {0.3, 1, 0.3, 2, 1} for others.

5.2 Summary Generation

We extract 30 candidate sentences with high S ordered by S from bigger to smaller and check them one by one. We use 30 sentences to make sure that when a candidate sentence is not good to be in a final summary, we could have enough other alternative sentences with less S. Then we generate the final summary as Figure 5.

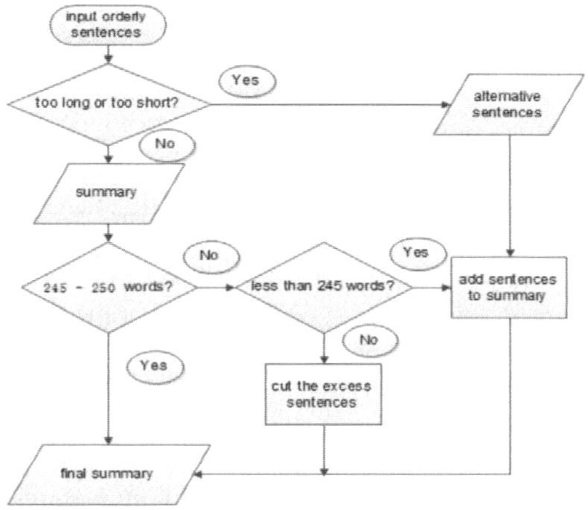

Figure 5: 250-summary generation flow chart

6 Evaluations

We've got only the automatic evaluation result. CIST could get best performance in some language, such as Hindi in ROUGE, and in some topics, such as Arabic M104, English and Romania M005, Czech M007, Spanish M103 etc. in N-gram graph methods: AutoSummENG, MeMoG and NPowER. CIST could also get nearly worst performance in some cases, such as French and Hebrew. In other cases it gets middle performance. But Chinese result looks very strange to us; we think that it needs more special discussion.

7 Conclusion and Future Work

hLDA is a language independent model. It could work well sometimes, but not stable enough. Future work will focus on parameter adjustment, modeling result evaluation, sentence evaluation and good summary generation.

Acknowledgments

We get support from NSFC 61202247, 71231002, Fundamental Research Funds for Central Universities 2013RC0304 and Beijing Science and Technology Information Institute.

[4] http://nlp.stanford.edu/software/CRF-NER.shtml

References

Abdullah Bawakid and Mourad Oussalah, 2008. *A Semantic Summarization System: University of Birmingham at TAC 2008. TAC 2008 Proceedings.*

Alistair Kennedy, Terry Copeck, Diana Inkpen and Stan Szpakowicz, 2010.*Entropy-based Sentence Selection with Roget's Thesaurus. TAC 2010 Proceedings.*

Annie Louis and Ani Nenkova, 2009. *Predicting Summary Quality using Limited Human Input. TAC 2009 Proceedings.*

Anton Leuski, Chin-Yewlin, Liang Zhou, Ulrich Germann, Franz Josef Och, and Eduard Hovy,2003. *Cross-Lingual C*ST*RD: English Access to Hindi Information. ACM Transactions on Asian Language Information Processing,* 2(3):245–269.

Arora Rachit, and Balaraman Ravindran, 2008. *Latent dirichlet allocation based multi-document summarization. Proceedings of the second workshop on Analytics for noisy unstructured text data. ACM, 2008.*

Asli Celikyilmaz and Dilek Hakkani-Tur. 2010. *A hybrid hierarchical model for multi-document summarization. Proceedings of the 48th Annual Meeting of the Association for Computational Linguistics,* 815–824, Uppsala, Sweden, 11-16 July 2010.

Blei D. and Lafferty J., 2006. *Dynamic topic models. In International Conference on Machine Learning (2006).* ACM, New York, NY, USA:113–120.

Blei D., Griffiths T. and Jordan M., 2010. *The nested Chinese restaurant process and Bayesian nonparametric inference of topic hierarchies. J. ACM* 57, 2 (2010):1–30.

Chin-Yew Lin and Eduard Hovy, 2002. *Automated Multi-document Summarization in NeATS. Proceedings of HLT 2002, Second International Conference on Human Language Technology Research.*

Chong Long, Minlie Huang and Xiaoyan Zhu, 2009. *Tsinghua University at TAC 2009: Summarizing Multi-documents by Information Distance. TAC 2009 Proceedings.*

D. M. Blei, A. Ng, and M. Jordan. 2003. *Latent dirichlet allocation, Jrnl. Machine Learning Research*, 3:993-1022, 2003b.

Feng Jin, Minlie Huang and Xiaoyan Zhu, 2010.*The THU Summarization Systems at TAC 2010. TAC 2010 Proceedings.*

Firas Hmida and Benoit Favre, 2011. *LIF at TAC Multiling: Towards a Truly Language Independent Summarizer. TAC 2011 Proceedings.*

Griffiths T., Steyvers M., Blei D. and Tenenbaum J., 2005. *Integrating topics and syntax. Advances in Neural Information Processing Systems 17.* L. K. Saul, Y. Weiss, and L. Bottou, eds. MIT Press, Cambridge, MA,2005:537–544.

Hongyan Liu, Ping'an Liu, Wei Heng and Lei Li, 2011.*The CIST Summarization System at TAC 2011. TAC 2011 Proceedings.*

Horacio Saggion, 2011. *Using SUMMA for Language Independent Summarization at TAC 2011. TAC 2011 Proceedings.*

John M. Conroy and Judith D. Schlesinger, 2008. *CLASSY and TAC 2008 Metrics. TAC 2008 Proceedings.*

John M. Conroy, Judith D. Schlesinger and Dianne P. O'Leary, 2006. *Topic-Focused Multi-document Summarization Using an Approximate Oracle Score. Proceedings of the COLING/ACL 2006 Main Conference Poster Sessions*: 152–159.

John M. Conroy, Judith D. Schlesinger and Jeff Kubina, 2011.*CLASSY 2011 at TAC: Guided and Multi-lingual Summaries and Evaluation Metrics. TAC 2011 Proceedings.*

Jorge García Flores, Laurent Gillard and Olivier Ferret, 2008. *Bag-of-senses versus bag-of-words: comparing semantic and lexical approaches on sentence extraction. TAC 2008 Proceedings.*

Josef Steinberger, Mijail Kabadjov, Ralf Steinberger, Hristo Tanev, Marco Turchi and Vanni Zavarella,2011. *JRC's Participation at TAC 2011: Guided and Multilingual Summarization Tasks. TAC 2011 Proceedings.*

Judith D. Schlesinger, Dianne P. O'Leary and John M. Conroy, 2008. *Arabic/English Multi-document Summarization with CLASSY—The Past and the Future. CICLing 2008 Proceedings*: 568–581.

Krestel Ralf, Peter Fankhauser and Wolfgang Nejdl, 2009. *Latent dirichlet allocation for tag recommendation. Proceedings of the third ACM conference on Recommender systems. ACM, 2009.*

Mahmoud El-Haj, Udo Kruschwitz and Chris Fox, 2011. *University of Essex at the TAC 2011 Multilingual Summarisation Pilot. TAC 2011 Proceedings.*

Niraj Kumar, Kannan Srinathan and Vasudeva Varma, 2010. *An Effective Approach for AESOP and Guided Summarization Task. TAC 2010 Proceedings.*

Pierre-Etienne Genest and Guy Lapalme, 2010.*Text Generation for Abstractive Summarization. TAC 2010 Proceedings.*

Pradipto Das and Rohini Srihari, 2011.*Global and Local Models for Multi-Document Summarization. TAC 2011 Proceedings.*

Renxian Zhang, You Ouyang and Wenjie Li, 2011.*Guided Summarization with Aspect Recognition. TAC 2011 Proceedings.*

Shih-Hsiang Lin and Berlin Chen, 2009. *THE NTNU SUMMARIZATION SYSTEM AT TAC 2009. TAC 2009 Proceedings.*

Shu Gong, Youli Qu and Shengfeng Tian, 2009. *Summarization using Wikipedia. TAC 2010 Proceedings.*

Sylvain Bellemare, Sabine Bergler and Ren´e Witte, 2008. *ERSS at TAC 2008. TAC 2008 Proceedings.*

Teh Y., Jordan M., Beal M. and Blei D., 2006. *Hierarchical Dirichlet processes. J. Am. Stat. Assoc.* 101, 476(2006):1566–1581.

Tingting He, Jinguang Chen, Zhuoming Gui, and Fang Li, 2008. *CCNU at TAC 2008 : Proceeding on Using Semantic Method for Automated Summarization Yield. TAC 2008 Proceedings.*

Wang C. and Blei D., 2009. *Decoupling sparsity and smoothness in the discrete hierarchical Dirichlet process. Advances in Neural Information Processing Systems 22.* Y. Bengio, D. Schuurmans, J. Lafferty, C.

William M. Darling, 2010. *Multi-Document Summarization from First Principles. TAC 2010 Proceedings.*

Xiaojun Wan, Jianwu Yang and Jianguo Xiao, 2006. *Using Cross-Document Random Walks for Topic-Focused Multi-Document Summarization. WI 2006 Main Conference Proceedings.*

Yuanrong Zheng and Tokunaga Takenobu, 2009. *The TITech Summarization System at TAC-2009. TAC 2009 Proceedings.*

Multilingual Multi-Document Summarization with POLY^2

Marina Litvak
Department of Software Engineering
Shamoon College of Engineering
Beer Sheva, Israel
marinal@sce.ac.il

Natalia Vanetik
Department of Software Engineering
Shamoon College of Engineering
Beer Sheva, Israel
natalyav@sce.ac.il

Abstract

In this paper we present a linear model for the problem of text summarization, where a summary preserves the information coverage as much as possible in comparison to the original document set. We reduce the problem of finding the best summary to the problem of finding the point on a convex polytope closest to the given hyperplane, and solve it efficiently with the help of fractional linear programming. We supply here an overview of our system, titled POLY^2, that participated in the MultiLing contest at ACL 2013.

1 Introduction

Automated text summarization is an active field of research in various communities like Information Retrieval (IR), Natural Language Processing (NLP), and Text Mining (TM).

Some authors reduce summarization to the maximum coverage problem (Takamura and Okumura, 2009; Gillick and Favre, 2009) that, despite a great performance, is known as NP-hard (Khuller et al., 1999). Linear Programming helps to find an accurate approximated solution to this problem and became very popular in summarization field in the last years (Gillick and Favre, 2009; Woodsend and Lapata, 2010; Hitoshi Nishikawa and Kikui, 2010; Makino et al., 2011). However, most mentioned works use exponential number of constraints.

Trying to solve a trade-off between summary quality and time complexity, we propose a novel summarization model solving the approximated maximum coverage problem by linear programming in polynomial time. We measure information coverage by terms[1] and strive to obtain a summary that preserves the optimal value of the chosen objective function as much as possible in comparison to the original document. Various objective functions combining different parameters like term's position and its frequency are introduced and evaluated.

Our method ranks and extracts significant sentences into a summary and it can be generalized for both single-document and multi-document summarization. Also, it can be easily adapted to cross-lingual/multilingual summarization.

Formally speaking, in this paper we introduce (1) a novel text representation model expanding a classic Vector Space Model (Salton et al., 1975) to Hyperplane and Half-spaces, (2) re-formulated extractive summarization problem as an optimization task and (3) its solution using linear programming. The main challenge of this paper is a new text representation model making possible to represent an exponential number of extracts without computing them explicitly, and finding the optimal one by simple minimizing a distance function in polynomial time.

2 Our Method

2.1 Definitions

We are given a set of sentences $S_1, ..., S_n$ derived from a document or a cluster of related documents. Meaningful words in these sentences are entirely described by terms $T_1, ..., T_m$. Our goal is to find a subset $S_{i_1}, ..., S_{i_k}$ consisting of sentences such that (1) there are at most N terms in these sentences, (2) term frequency is preserved as much as possible w.r.t. the original sentence set, (3) redundant information among k selected sentences is minimized.

We use the standard sentence-term matrix, $A = (a_{ij})$ of size $m \times n$, for initial data representation, where $a_{ij} = k$ if term T_i appears in the sentence S_j precisely k times.

Our goal is to find subset $i_1, ..., i_k$ of A's

[1] normalized meaningful words

columns so that the chosen submatrix represents the best possible summary under some constraints. Since it is hard to determine what is the best summary mathematically (this task is usually left to human experts), we wish to express summary quality as a linear function of the underlying matrix. We strive to find a summary that gives an optimal value once the function in question has been determined.

Basic text preprocessing includes sentence splitting and tokenization. Also, additional steps like stopwords removal, stemming, synonym resolution, etc. may be performed for resource-rich languages.

2.2 Polytope as a document representation

We represent every sentence by a hyperplane and the lower half-space of that hyperplane. In a way, the hyperplane bounding each half-space is the sentence itself, and a half-space below it is an approximation of that sentence. An intersection of lower half-spaces in Euclidean space forms a convex polyhedron, and in our case the faces of this polyhedron are intersections of hyperplanes bounding lower half-spaces that stand for document sentences. We add trivial constraints so that the polyhedron representing the entire document is bounded, i.e. is a *polytope*. All possible extracts from the document can be represented by hyperplane intersections. Thus the boundary of the resulting polytope is a good approximation for extracts that can be generated from the given document.

We view every column of the sentence-term matrix as a *linear constraint* representing a lower half-space in $\mathbb{R}^{mn}$. An occurrence of term t_i in sentence S_j is represented by variable x_{ij}. The maximality constraint on the number of terms in the summary can be easily expressed as a constraint on the sum of these variables. Note that each sentence constraint uses its n unique variables, thus making sure that the intersection of every subset of sentence hyperplane is not empty and is well-defined.

Every sentence S_j in our document is a lower half-space of a hyperlane in $\mathbb{R}^{mn}$, defined with columns of A and variables $x_{1j}, \ldots, x_{mj}$ representing the terms in this sentence:

$$\begin{gathered} A[][j] = [a_{1j}, \ldots, a_{mj}] \\ \mathbf{x}_j = [x_{1j}, \ldots, x_{mj}] \text{ for all } 1 \leq j \leq n \end{gathered}$$

We define a system of linear inequalities

$$\begin{aligned} A[][j] \cdot \mathbf{x}_j^T = \textstyle\sum_{i=1}^m a_{ij} x_{ij} \leq \\ \leq A[][j] \cdot \mathbf{1}^T = \textstyle\sum_{i=1}^m a_{ij} \end{aligned} \tag{1}$$

Every inequality of this form defines a lower half-space of a hyperplane

$$H_i := (A[][j] \cdot \mathbf{x}_j^T = A[][j] \cdot \mathbf{1}^T)$$

To say that every term is either present or absent from the chosen extract, we add constraints $0 \leq x_{ij} \leq 1$. Intuitively, the entire hyperplane H_i and therefore every point $p \in H_i$ represents sentence S_i. Then a subset of r sentences is represented by intersection of r hyperplanes.

2.3 Summary constraints

We express summarization constraints in the form of linear inequalities. Maximality constraint on the number of terms in the summary can be easily expressed as a constraint on the sum of all term variables x_{ij}, and the same goes for minimality constraint.

2.4 The polytope model

Having defined linear inequalities that describe each sentence in a document separately and the total number of terms in sentence subset, we can now look at them together as a system:

$$\begin{cases} \sum_{i=1}^m a_{i1} x_{i1} \leq \sum_{i=1}^m a_{i1} \\ \ldots \\ \sum_{i=1}^m a_{in} x_{in} \leq \sum_{i=1}^m a_{in} \\ T_{\min} \leq \sum_{i=1}^m \sum_{j=1}^n x_{ij} \leq T_{\max} \\ W_{\min} \leq \sum_{i=1}^m \sum_{j=1}^n a_{ij} x_{ij} \leq W_{\max} \\ 0 \leq x_{ij} \leq 1 \end{cases} \tag{2}$$

First n inequalities describe sentences $S_1, \ldots, S_n$, the next two inequalities describes constraints on the total number of terms and words in a summary, and the final constraint determines upper and lower boundaries for all sentence-term variables. Intersections of $S_1, \ldots, S_n$ are well-defined, since every pair of sentences is described by a linear constraints on different n-tuple of variables x_{ij} out of total mn variables. Since every inequality in the system (2) is linear, the entire system describes a convex polyhedron, which we denote by $\mathbf{P}$.

2.5 Objectives and summary extraction

We assume here that the surface of the polyhedron $\mathbf{P}$ is a suitable representation of all the possible

Function	Formula	Description
Maximal Weighted Term Sum (OBJ_1)	max $\sum_{i=1}^{m} w_i t_i$, $t_i = \sum_{j=1}^{n} x_{ji}$	Maximizes the information coverage as a weighted term sum. We used the following types of term weights w_i. (1) POS_EQ, where $w_i = 1$ for all i; (2) POS_F, where $w_i = \frac{1}{app(i)}$ and $app(i)$ is the index of a sentence in the document where the term T_i first appeared; (3) POS_B, where $w_i = \max\{\frac{1}{app(i)}, \frac{1}{n-app(i)+1}\}$; (4) TF, where $w_i = \text{tf}(i)$ and $\text{tf}(i)$ is the term frequency of term T_i; (5) TFISF, where $w_i = \text{tf}(i) * \text{isf}(i)$ and $isf(i)$ is the inverse sentence frequency of T_i
Distance Function (OBJ_2)	min $\sum_{i=1}^{m} (\widehat{t_i} - p_i)^2$, (1) $\widehat{t_i} = t_i = \sum_{j=1}^{n} x_{ji}$ and $\forall i\ p_i = 1$, or (2) $\widehat{t_i} = \frac{t_i}{\sum_{j=1}^{m} t_j}$ and $p_i = \text{tf}(i)$	Minimizes the Eucledian distance between terms $t = (t_1, \ldots, t_m)$ (a point on the polytope **P** representing a generated summary) and the vector $p = (p_1, \ldots, p_m)$ (expressing document properties we wish to preserve and representing the "ideal" summary). We used the following options for t and p representation. (1) MTC, where t is a summary term count vector and p contains all the terms precisely once, thus minimizing repetition but increasing terms coverage. (2) MTF, where t contains term frequency of terms in a summary and p contains term frequency for terms in documents.
Sentence Overlap (OBJ_3)	min $\sum_{j=1}^{n} \sum_{k=j+1}^{n} ovl_{jk}$, $ovl_{jk} = \frac{\lvert S_j \cap S_k \rvert}{\lvert S_j \cup S_k \rvert} = \frac{\sum_{i=1}^{m} w(a_{ij}, a_{ik})(x_{ij} + x_{ik})}{\sum_{i=1}^{m} (a_{ij} + a_{ik})}$	Minimizes the Jaccard similarity between sentences in a summary (denoted by ovl_{jk} for S_j and S_k). $w(a_{ij}, a_{ik})$ is 1 if the term T_i is present in both sentences S_j and S_k and is 0 otherwise.
Maximal Bigram Sum (OBJ_4)	max $\sum_{i,j} \text{bi}_{ij}$, where $\forall i, j\ 0 \le \text{bi}_{ij} \le 1$	Maximizes the information coverage as a bigram sum. Variable bi_{ij} is defined for every bigram (T_i, T_j) in the text.

Table 1: Objective functions for summarization using polytope model.

sentence subsets. Fortunately, we do not need to scan the whole set of **P**'s surfaces but rather to find the point on **P** that optimizes the chosen objective function. Table 1 contains four different objective functions that we used for summarization, along with descriptions of the changes in the model that were required for each function.

Since fractional LP method not only finds the optimal value of objective function but also presents an evidence to that optimality in the form of a point $x = (x_{ij})$, we use the point's data to find what sentences belong to the chosen summary. The point x may satisfy several of the sentence inequalities as equalities, while other inequalities may not turn into equalities. If sentence inequality is turned into equality by x, the sentence necessarily belongs to the chosen summary. Otherwise, the point x that optimizes the chosen objective function represents a summary that does not contain sufficient number of words or terms. In this case we add additional sentences to the summary and we choose these sentences on the basis of their distance from the point x. Sentence hyperplanes that are the nearest to the point x are chosen in a greedy manner and added to the summary. This test is straightforward and takes $O(mn)$ time.

3 POLY^2: system description

We title our system POLY^2 as a double POLY occured in "POLYnomial Summarization using POLYtope model". POLY^2 is implemented in Java and it uses lp-solve software (Berkelaar, 1999) in order to perform Linear Programming. The input for our system is initial collection of texts to be summarized. Four main parts of POLY^2 are: preprocessing, linear program generation, linear program application and testing. Data flow of the system is depicted in Figure 1.

The **preprocessing step** consists of following parts. During the very first step, initial documents undergo stop word removal, stemming and synonym resolution (if available for the chosen language). Then, a sentence-term matrix is generated in the form of a text file, where every line describes a term and every column – a sentence. Also, the index list for multi-document summarization is generated. In this list serial number of each sentence is paired up with its serial number in its document. This information is used later in order to decide how close each sentence is to its document's boundaries. Finally, we generate list of bigrams (a consecutive appearance of two terms) for every sentence. All of the files gener-

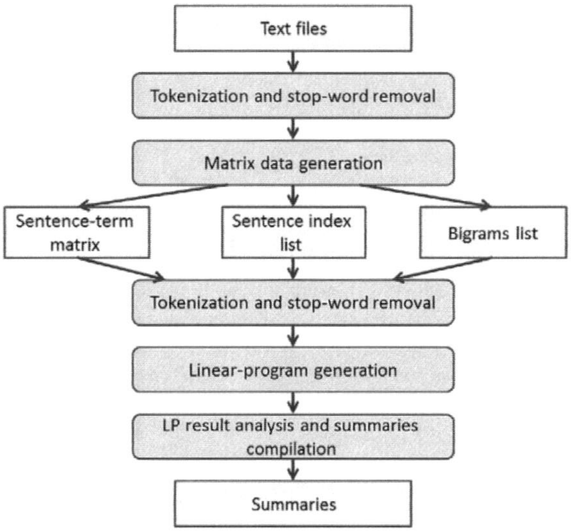

Figure 1: Data flow of the POLY^2 system.

```
max :
tm0+tm1+tm2+tm3+tm4+tm5+tm6+tm7+tm8+tm9+tm10+tm11+tm12
10tm0=tx0_0+tx0_12+tx0_38+tx0_45+tx0_50+tx0_55+tx0_63+tx0_92+
tm1=tx1_0;
tm2=tx2_0;
tm3=tx3_0;
tm4=tx4_0;
tm5=tx5_0;
64tm6=tx6_0+tx6_6+tx6_12+tx6_17+tx6_18+tx6_19+tx6_20+tx6_21+t
tm7=tx7_0;
tm8=tx8_0;
tm9=tx9_0;
tm10=tx10 0;
```

Figure 2: Linear program generated by POLY^2 system.

ated during preprocessing are text files.

The main part of POLY^2 is **linear program generation**. The system allows to select document matrix files and auxiliary files and objective function and generates a system of linear inequalities together with an objective function in format acceptable by lp-solve software. Figure 2 shows a sample LP file contents. Note that file generation for every one of our objective function takes only seconds for a single documents.

The next step is to **run linear program** and extract its results. We use lp-solve Java API to perform this task and extract coordinates of point x that optimizes the chosen objective function. In order to construct the summary, we measure the normalized distance from point x to every one of the sentence hyperplanes. Since this information is readily available through lp-solve API, the task requires sorting of n real numbers, where n is the number of sentences in all of the documents together. Hyperplanes whose distance to x is minimal represent the sentences participating in the final summary. Running time of this step for a single file does not exceed three seconds.

The final (optional) step is to verify generated summaries, that can be performed with the help of any evaluation system. In our case, the ROUGE (Lin, 2004) system has been used.

4 Conclusions and Future Work

In this paper we present an extractive summarization system POLY^2 based on a linear programming model. We represent the document as a set of intersecting hyperplanes. Every possible summary of a document is represented as the intersection of two or more hyperlanes. We consider the summary to be the best if the optimal value of objective function is preserved during summarization, and translate the summarization problem into a problem of finding a point on a convex polytope which is the closest to the hyperplane describing the "ideal" summary. We introduce multiple objective functions describing the distance between a summary (a point on a convex polytope) and the best summary (the hyperplane). Since the introduced objectives behaves differently on different languages, only two of them were indicated as primary systems and evaluated by MultiLing 2013 organizers–$OBJ_1^{POS\_F}$ and OBJ_3–denoted by ID5 and ID51.

Below we summarize the results of automated evaluations in MultiLing 2013 (ROUGE-1,2,3,4 and three N-gram graph methods) for POLY^2 in three languages.

English: 7th place in all ROUGE metrics (stemmed) and AutoSummENG, and 8th place in MeMoG and NPowER (out of 10 systems);

Hebrew: 3rd place in ROUGE-1, 5th place in ROUGE-2 and MeMoG, 4th rank in ROUGE-3 and ROUGE-4, and only 6th rank in terms of AutoSummENG and NPowER (out of 9 participants);

Arabic: 7th rank in ROUGE-1,2 and all NGG metrics, 6th rank in terms of ROUGE-3, and 5th place in ROUGE-4 (out of 10 summarizers).

As it can be seen, the best performance for POLY^2 has been achieved on the dataset of Hebrew documents.

Since fractional linear programming problem can be solved in polynomial time (Karmarkar, 1984), the time complexity of our approach is polynomial.

Acknowledgments

Authors thank Igor Vinokur for the software maintenance and running of experiments.

References

Michel Berkelaar. 1999. lp-solve free software. `http://lpsolve.sourceforge.net/5.5/`.

Dan Gillick and Benoit Favre. 2009. A Scalable Global Model for Summarization. In *Proceedings of the NAACL HLT Workshop on Integer Linear Programming for Natural Language Processing*, pages 10–18.

Yoshihiro Matsuo Hitoshi Nishikawa, Takaaki Hasegawa and Genichiro Kikui. 2010. Opinion Summarization with Integer Linear Programming Formulation for Sentence Extraction and Ordering. In *Coling 2010: Poster Volume*, pages 910–918.

N. Karmarkar. 1984. New polynomial-time algorithm for linear programming. *Combinatorica*, 4:373–395.

L. G. Khachiyan and M. J. Todd. 1993. On the complexity of approximating the maximal inscribed ellipsoid for a polytope. *Mathematical Programming*, 61:137–159.

L. G. Khachiyan. 1996. Rounding of polytopes in the real number model of computation. *Mathematics of Operations Research*, 21:307–320.

Samir Khuller, Anna Moss, and Joseph (Seffi) Naor. 1999. The budgeted maximum coverage problem. *Information Precessing Letters*, 70(1):39–45.

Chin-Yew Lin. 2004. Rouge: a package for automatic evaluation of summaries. In *Workshop on Text Summarization Branches Out, Post-Conference Workshop of ACL 2004*, pages 25–26.

Takuya Makino, Hiroya Takamura, and Manabu Okumura. 2011. Balanced coverage of aspects for text summarization. In *TAC '11: Proceedings of Text Analysis Conference*.

G. Salton, C. Yang, and A. Wong. 1975. A vector-space model for information retrieval. *Communications of the ACM*, 18.

Hiroya Takamura and Manabu Okumura. 2009. Text summarization model based on maximum coverage problem and its variant. In *EACL '09: Proceedings of the 12th Conference of the European Chapter of the Association for Computational Linguistics*, pages 781–789.

Kristian Woodsend and Mirella Lapata. 2010. Automatic Generation of Story Highlights. In *ACL '10: Proceedings of the 48th Annual Meeting of the Association for Computational Linguistics*, pages 565–574.

The UWB Summariser at Multiling-2013

Josef Steinberger
University of West Bohemia
Faculty of Applied Sciences
Department of Computer Science and Engineering, NTIS Centre
Univerzitni 8, 30614 Plzeň, Czech Republic
jstein@kiv.zcu.cz

Abstract

The paper describes our participation in the Multi-document summarization task of Multiling-2013. The community initiative was born as a pilot task for the Text Analysis Conference in 2011. This year the corpus was extended by new three languages and another five topics, covering in total 15 topics in 10 languages. Our summariser is based on latent semantic analysis and it is in principle language independent. Its results on the Multiling-2011 corpus were promising. The generated summaries were ranked first in several languages based on various metrics. The summariser with minor changes was run on the updated 2013 corpus. Although we do not have the manual evaluation results yet the ROUGE-2 score indicates good results again. The summariser produced best summaries in 6 from 10 considered languages according to the ROUGE-2 metric.

1 Introduction

Multi-document summarization has received increasing attention during the last decade. This was mainly due to the requirement of news monitoring to reduce the big bulk of highly redundant news data. More and more interest arises for approaches that will be able to be applied on a variety of languages. The summariser should be of high quality. However, when applied in a highly multilingual environment, it has to be enough language-independent to guarantee similar performance across languages.

Given the lack of multilingual summarisation evaluation resources, the summarisation community started to discuss the topic at Text Analysis Conference (TAC[1]) 2010. It resulted in the first multilingual shared task organised as part of TAC 2011 – Multiling-2011 (Giannakopoulos et al., 2012). Each group took an active role in the creation of their language subcorpus. Because no freely available parallel corpus suitable for multi-document summarisation was found, news clusters from WikiNews (in English) needed to be first translated to six other languages. Three model summaries for each cluster were then written and both model and peer summaries were manually evaluated. For Multiling-2013, three new languages were added (Chinese, Romanian and Spanish) and 5 new topics (news clusters) were added to the corpus.

This article contains the description of our system based on latent semantic analysis (LSA) which participated in Multiling-2013. We first briefly discuss the multi-document task in section 2. Then we show our summarisation approach based on LSA (Section 3). The next section (4) compares the participating systems based on the ROUGE-2 score. Manually assigned scores were not available at the time of creation of this report. We conclude by a discussion of possible improvements of the method which require language-specific resources.

2 Multi-document summarisation task at Multiling'13

MultiLing-2013 is a community effort, a set of research tasks and a corresponding workshop which covers three summarisation tasks, focused on the multilingual aspect. It aims to evaluate the application of (partially or fully) language-independent summarization algorithms on a variety of languages.

The annotation part consisted of four phases. The first phase was to select English WikiNews articles about the same event and to create the topics. The articles were then manually translated to the other languages. Model summaries were created

[1] http://www.nist.gov/tac/

separately for each language by native speakers. In a certain time frame, participating groups ran their summarisers and the automatic summaries were then evaluated, both manually (on a 5-to-1 scale) and automatically by ROUGE (Lin, 2004) and the AutoSummENG metric (Giannakopoulos and Karkaletsis, 2010).

We participated with our summariser in the main multi-document task, which requires to generate a single, fluent, representative summary from a set of 10 documents describing an event sequence. The language of the document set (topic) was within a given range of 10 languages (Arabic, Chinese, Czech, English, French, Greek, Hebrew, Hindi, Romanian and Spanish) and all documents in a set share the same language. The output summary should be of the same language as its source documents. The output summary should be 250 words at most. The corpus was extended to 15 topics (Chinese, French and Hindi subcorpora contained only 10 topics).

3 LSA-based summarisation approach

Originally proposed by Gong and Liu (2002) and later improved by Steinberger and Ježek (2004), this approach first builds a term-by-sentence matrix from the source, then applies Singular Value Decomposition (SVD) and finally uses the resulting matrices to identify and extract the most salient sentences. SVD finds the latent (orthogonal) dimensions, which in simple terms correspond to the different topics discussed in the source.

More formally, we first build matrix $\mathbf{A}$ where each column represents the weighted term-frequency vector of a sentence in a given set of documents. The weighting scheme we found to work best is using a binary local weight and an entropy-based global weight (for details see Steinberger and Ježek (2009)).

After that step Singular Value Decomposition (SVD) is applied to the above matrix as $\mathbf{A} = \mathbf{USV}^T$, and subsequently matrix $\mathbf{F} = \mathbf{S} \cdot \mathbf{V}^T$ reduced to r dimensions[2] is derived.

Sentence selection starts with measuring the length of sentence vectors in matrix $\mathbf{F}$ computed as the Euclidean norm. The length of the vector (the sentence score) can be viewed as a measure for importance of that sentence within the top cluster topics.

The sentence with the largest score is selected as the first to go to the summary (its corresponding vector in $\mathbf{F}$ is denoted as $\mathbf{f}_{best}$). After placing it in the summary, the topic/sentence distribution in matrix $\mathbf{F}$ is changed by subtracting the information contained in that sentence:

$$\mathbf{F}^{(it+1)} = \mathbf{F}^{(it)} - \frac{\mathbf{f}_{best} \cdot \mathbf{f}_{best}^T}{|\mathbf{f}_{best}|^2} \cdot \mathbf{F}^{(it)}. \qquad (1)$$

The vector lengths of similar sentences are decreased, thus preventing within summary redundancy. After the subtraction of information in the selected sentence, the process continues with the sentence which has the largest score computed on the updated matrix $\mathbf{F}$. The process is iteratively repeated until the required summary length is reached.

4 Experiments and results

Although the approach works only with term co-occurrence, and thus it is completely language-independent, pre-processing plays an important role and greatly affects the performance. When generating the summaries for Multiling-2013 each article was split into sentences. We used the old DUC sentence splitter[3], although a different sentence-splitting character was used for Chinese. It was a simplification because the sentence splitter should be adapted for each language (e.g. a different list of abbreviations should be used or language specific features should be added). If LSA is applied on a large matrix stopwords can be found in the first linear combination which could be then filtered out. However, in our case we apply it on rather small matrices and stopwords could affect negatively the topic distribution. Thus the safer option is to filter them out. This brings a dependency on a language but, on the other hand, acquiring lists of stop-words for various languages is not difficult. Filtering these insignificant terms does not also slow down the system. The stopwords were filtered out for all the languages of Multiling. The approach discussed in section 3 was then used to select sentences until the required summary length (250 words) has not been reached. Sentence order is important for event-based stories. In the case of the Multiling corpus,

[2]The degree of importance of each 'latent' topic is given by the singular values and the optimal number of latent topics (i.e., dimensions) r can be fine-tuned on training data. Our previous experiments led us to set r to 8% from the number of sentences for 250-word summaries.

[3]http://duc.nist.gov/duc2004/software/duc2003.breakSent.tar.gz

Language	Topics	Avg. Model	ID1	ID11	ID2	ID21	ID3	**ID4 (rank/total)**	ID5	ID51	Baseline
Arabic	15	.137	.132	.132	.118	.105	.052	**.167 (1/9)**	.105	.088	.086
Chinese	10	.462	.430	.457	.212	.354		**.354 (5/6)**			.867
Czech	15	.195	.155	.166	.123	.151		*.179 (1/6)*			.085
English	15	.185	.161	.161	.147	.142	.083	**.171 (1/9)**	.117	.101	.118
French	10	.198	.201	.201	.166	.177		**.214 (1/6)**			.130
Greek	15	.111	.120	.124	.100	.112		**.110 (4/6)**			.088
Hebrew	15	.076	.088	.100	.076	.084		**.092 (2/8)**	.087	.084	.072
Hindi	10	.342	.125	.132	.123	.123		**.129 (2/6)**			.114
Romanian	15	.543	.147	.139	.120	.138		**.166 (1/6)**			.098
Spanish	15	.239	.198	.218	.180	.175		**.228 (1/6)**			.164
Avg. rank			2.7	1.9	5.0	4.3	9	**1.9**	5.7	7.0	5.9

Table 1: ROUGE-2 scores of the average model and paricipating systems. Our LSA-based system is ID4 and we report its rank from the total number of systems which submitted summaries for the particular language. We included the baseline (the start of a centroid article) and excluded the topline which uses model sentences.

much attention has to be given to sentence ordering because some topics contained articles spread over a long period, even 5 years. We did not perform any temporal analysis at sentence level. The sentences in the summary were ordered based on the date of the article they came from. Sentences from the same article followed their order in the full text. Even if they were sometimes out of context, when extracted, the adjacent sentences at least dealt with the same (or temporary close) event.

We analysed ROUGE scores which we received from the organisers. We discuss here ROUGE-2 (bigram) score, a traditionally used metric in summarisation evaluation (Table 1). ROUGE-2 ranked our summariser on the top of the list for 6 from 10 languages (Arabic, Czech, English, French, Romanian, Spanish). System ID11 performed better twice (Hebrew and Hindi), there were three better systems in Greek and the baseline won in Chinese. In the following, we will discuss the results for each language separately.

For **Arabic**, our system received the best ROUGE-2 score. It was significantly better (at confidence 95%) then 5 other systems, including baseline. It performed on the same level as models.

It was our first attempt to run the summariser on **Chinese**. We did not use any specific word-splitting tool and we considered each character to be a context feature for LSA. The ROUGE results say that the summariser was not that successful compared to the others. It was significantly better than one system and worse than two and the baseline which received suspiciously high score.

We annotated the **Czech** part of the corpus, and therefore the result of our system can be considered only as another baseline for this language. It received the largest ROUGE-2 score, however, there was no significant difference among the top four systems.

For **English**, our system together with the following systems ID1 and ID11 were significantly better than the rest. A similar conclusion can be driven by observing the **French** results. In the case of **Greek** only baseline performed poorly. Our approach was ranked fourth although there were marginal differences between the systems. For **Hebrew** and **Hindi** system ID11 performed the best, followed by our system. For **Romanian**, a newly introduced language this year, our system received a high score, however, a larger confidence interval did not show much significance. For another newly-introduced language, **Spanish**, only system ID11 was not significantly worse than our system.

As a try to compare the systems across languages, an average rank was computed. (Computing an average of absolute ROUGE-2 scores did not seem to have sense.) Our system and system ID11 received the best average rank: 1.9.

For several languages (Arabic, French, Hebrew), our summaries were better (not significantly) then the average model according to ROUGE-2.

The AutoSummENG method (Giannakopoulos and Karkaletsis, 2010) gave results similar to those of ROUGE. The only difference was in Chinese: ROUGE-2 ranked our system 5th, AutoSummENG 1st.

One question remains: are the ROUGE scores correlated with human grades? Unfortunately, the human grades were not available at the time of the system reports submission. However, because we were managing annotation of the Czech subcorpus we had access to human grades for that language. The system ranking provided by ROUGE mostly agree with the human grades, reaching Pearson correlation of .97 for the systems-only scenario. The human grades ranked our system as significantly better than any other submission in the case of Czech.

5 Conclusion

The evaluation indicates good results of our summariser, mainly for European Latin-script languages (Czech, English, French, Romanian and Spanish). It could be connected to good-enough pre-processing (sentence and word splitting). The last two languages were added this year and the good results show that the LSA-based summariser can produce good summaries when run on an 'unseen' language.

We experiment with several improvements of the method which require language-specific resources. Entity detection can improve the LSA model by adding entity features as new rows in the SVD input matrix (Steinberger et al., 2007). From the Multiling-2013 languages we have developed the NER tool only for 6 languages (Arabic, Czech, English, French, Romanian and Spanish) so far (Pouliquen and Steinberger, 2009). A coreference- (anaphora-) resolution can help in checking and rewriting the entity references in a summary (Steinberger et al., 2007) although there is usually a high dependency on the language (e.g. in the case of pronouns).

Event extraction can detect important aspects related to the category of the topic (e.g. detecting victims in a topic about an accident) (Steinberger et al., 2011). The aspect information can be used in the model weighting or during sentence selection. We have developed the tool for 5 languages considered in Multiling-2013 (Arabic, Czech, English, French and Spanish). Temporal analysis could improve sentence ordering if a correct temporal mark, which contains information about time of a discussed event, is attached to each summary sentence (Steinberger et al., 2012).

So far, we experimented with English, French and Spanish from the list of the Multiling languages. By compressing and/or rephrasing the saved space in the summary could be filled in by the next most salient sentences, and thus the summary can cover more content from the source texts. We have already tried to investigate language-independent possibilities in that direction (Turchi et al., 2010).

Acknowledgments

This work was supported by project "NTIS - New Technologies for Information Society", European Center of Excellence, CZ.1.05/1.1.00/02.0090.

References

G. Giannakopoulos and V. Karkaletsis. 2010. Summarization system evaluation variations based on n-gram graphs. In *Proceedings of the Text Analysis Conference (TAC)*.

G. Giannakopoulos, M. El-Haj, B. Favre, M. Litvak, J. Steinberger, and V. Varma. 2012. Tac 2011 multiling pilot overview. In *Proceedings of the Text Analysis Conference (TAC)*. NIST.

Y. Gong and X. Liu. 2002. Generic text summarization using relevance measure and latent semantic analysis. In *Proceedings of ACM SIGIR*, New Orleans, US.

C.-Y. Lin. 2004. ROUGE: a package for automatic evaluation of summaries. In *Proceedings of the Workshop on Text Summarization Branches Out*, Barcelona, Spain.

B. Pouliquen and R. Steinberger. 2009. Automatic construction of multilingual name dictionaries. In Cyril Goutte, Nicola Cancedda, Marc Dymetman, and George Foster, editors, *Learning Machine Translation*. MIT Press, NIPS series.

J. Steinberger and K. Ježek. 2004. Text summarization and singular value decomposition. In *Proceedings of the 3rd ADVIS conference*, Izmir, Turkey.

J. Steinberger and K. Ježek. 2009. Update summarization based on novel topic distribution. In *Proceedings of the 9th ACM Symposium on Document Engineering, Munich, Germany*.

J. Steinberger, M. Poesio, M. Kabadjov, and K. Ježek. 2007. Two uses of anaphora resolution in summarization. *Information Processing and Management*, 43(6):1663–1680. Special Issue on Text Summarisation (Donna Harman, ed.).

J. Steinberger, H. Tanev, M. Kabadjov, and R. Steinberger. 2011. Aspect-driven news summarization. *International Journal of Computational Linguistics and Applications*, 2(1-2).

J. Steinberger, M. Kabadjov, R. Steinberger, H. Tanev, M. Turchi, and V. Zavarella. 2012. Towards language-independent news summarization. In *Proceedings of the Text Analysis Conference (TAC)*. NIST.

M. Turchi, J. Steinberger, M. Kabadjov, R. Steinberger, and N. Cristianini. 2010. Wrapping up a summary: from representation to generation. In *Proceedings of CLEF*.

Multilingual Summarization: Dimensionality Reduction and a Step Towards Optimal Term Coverage

John M. Conroy
IDA / Center for Computing Sciences
conroy@super.org

Sashka T. Davis
IDA / Center for Computing Sciences
stdavi3@super.org

Jeff Kubina
Department of Defense
jmkubin@tycho.ncsc.mil

Yi-Kai Liu
National Institute of Standards and Technology
yi-kai.liu@nist.gov

Dianne P. O'Leary
University of Maryland and NIST
oleary@cs.umd.edu

Judith D. Schlesinger
IDA/Center for Computing Sciences
drj1945@gmail.com

Abstract

In this paper we present three term weighting approaches for multi-lingual document summarization and give results on the DUC 2002 data as well as on the 2013 Multilingual Wikipedia feature articles data set. We introduce a new interval-bounded nonnegative matrix factorization. We use this new method, latent semantic analysis (LSA), and latent Dirichlet allocation (LDA) to give three term-weighting methods for multi-document multi-lingual summarization. Results on DUC and TAC data, as well as on the MultiLing 2013 data, demonstrate that these methods are very promising, since they achieve oracle coverage scores in the range of humans for 6 of the 10 test languages. Finally, we present three term weighting approaches for the MultiLing13 single document summarization task on the Wikipedia featured articles. Our submissions significantly outperformed the baseline in 19 out of 41 languages.

1 Our Approach to Single and Multi-Document Summarization

The past 20 years of research have yielded a bounty of successful methods for single document summarization (SDS) and multi-document summarization (MDS). Techniques from statistics, machine learning, numerical optimization, graph theory, and combinatorics are generally language-independent and have been applied both to single and multi-document extractive summarization of multi-lingual data.

In this paper we extend the work of our research group, most recently discussed in Davis et al. (2012) for multi-document summarization, and apply it to both single and multi-document multi-lingual document summarization. Our extractive multi-document summarization performs the following steps:

1. Sentence boundary detection;
2. Tokenization and term identification;
3. Term-sentence matrix generation;
4. Term weight determination;
5. Sentence selection;
6. Sentence ordering.

Sentence boundary detection and tokenization are language dependent, while steps (3)-(6) are language independent. We briefly discuss each of these steps.

We use a rule based *sentence splitter* FASST-E (very Fast, very Accurate Sentence Splitter for Text – English) (Conroy et al., 2009) and its multi-lingual extensions (Conroy et al., 2011) for determining the boundary of individual sentences.

Proper *tokenization* improves the quality of the summary and may include stemming and also morphological analysis to disambiguate compound words in languages such as Arabic. Tokenization may also include stop word removal. The result of this step is that each sentence is represented as a sequence of terms, where a term can be a single word, a sequence of words, or character n-grams. The specifics of tokenization are discussed in Section 2.

Matrix generation (the vector space model) was pioneered by Salton (1991). Later Dumais (1994) introduced dimensionality reduction in document retrieval systems, and this approach has also been used by many researchers for document summarization. (In addition to our own work, see, for example Steinberger and Jezek (2009).) We construct a single term-sentence matrix $A = (a_{i,j})$, where $i = 1, \ldots, m$ ranges over all terms, and $j = 1, \ldots, n$ ranges over all sentences, for either a single document, when we perform SDS, or for a collection of documents for MDS. The row labels of the term-sentence matrix are the terms $T = (t_1, \ldots, t_m)$ determined after tokenization. The column labels are the sentences $S_1, \ldots, S_n$ of the document(s). The entries of the matrix A are defined by

$$a_{i,j} = \ell_{i,j} g_i,$$

Here, $\ell_{i,j}$ is the local weight, which is 1 when term i appears in sentence j and 0 otherwise.

The *global weight* g_i should be proportional to the contribution of the term in describing the major themes of the document. While the global weight could be used as a *term weight* in a sentence selection scheme, it may be beneficial to perform dimensionality reduction on the matrix A and compute term weights based on the lower dimensional matrix. In this work we seek to find strong term weights for both single- and and multi-document summarization. These cases are handled separately, as we found that multi-document summarization benefits a lot from dimensionality reduction while single document summarization does not.

Our previous multi-document summarization algorithm, OCCAMS (Davis et al., 2012), used the linear algebraic technique of Latent Semantic Analysis (LSA) to determine term weights and used techniques from combinatorial optimization for sentence selection. In our CLASSY algorithms (e.g., (Conroy et al., 2011)), we used both a language model and machine learning as two alternative approaches to assign term weights. CLASSY then used linear algebraic techniques or an integer linear program for sentence selection. Section 3 describes the term weights we use when we summarize single documents. In Section 4 we present three different dimensionality reduction techniques for the term-sentence matrix A.

Once term weight learning has assigned weights for each term of the document(s) and dimensionality reduction has been applied (if desired), the next step, *sentence selection*, chooses a set of sentences of maximal length L for the extract summary. These sentences should cover the major themes of the document(s), minimize redundancy, and satisfy the bound on the length of the summary. We discuss our OCCAMS_V sentence selection algorithm in Section 5.

Sentence ordering is performed using an approximate traveling salesperson algorithm (Conroy et al., 2009).

Three term weighting variants were used to generate summaries for each of the 10 languages in the MultiLing 2013 multi-document summarization task. The target summary length was set to be 250 words for all languages except Chinese, where 700 characters were generated.

We now present the details of our improvements to our algorithms and results of our experiments.

2 From Text to Term-Sentence Matrix

After sentence boundaries are determined, we used one of three simple tokenization methods and then one of two term-creation methods, as summarized in Table 1. Languages were divided into three categories: English, non-English languages with space delimited words, and ideographic languages (Chinese for MDS and Chinese, Japanese, and Thai for the SDS pilot task). For non-ideographic languages, tokens are formed based on a regular expression. For English, tokens are defined as contiguous sequences of upper or lower case letters and numbers. For other non-ideographic languages, tokens were defined similarly, and the regular expression describes what characters are used to break the tokens. These characters include white space and most punctuation except the apostrophe. For English, Porter stemming was used for both SDS and MDS, with a stop list of approximately 600 words for SDS. For English and other word-based languages, lower-cased bi-tokens were used in MDS and lower-cased tokens for SDS. For all languages, and both SDS and MDS, Dunning's mutual information statistic (Dunning, 1993) is used to select terms, using the other documents as background. The p-value (rejection threshold), initially set at 5.0e-4, is repeatedly doubled until the number of terms is at least twice the length of the target summary (250 for MDS, 150 words or 500 characters for SDS). Note that these terms are high confidence signature terms (Lin and Hovy, 2000) i.e., the p-value is small. We describe our terms as high mutual information (HMI), since Dunning's statistic is equivalent to mutual information as defined by

Language	Tokens	Terms for MDS	Terms for SDS
English	[^A-Za-z0-9]	HMI bi-tokens	HMI non-stop-word tokens
Non-English	`[\s.?,";:~![](){}<>&⋆=+@#$]`	HMI bi-tokens	HMI tokens
Ideographic	4-byte grams	HMI tokens	HMI tokens

Table 1: Term and token definition as a function of language and task.

Cover and Thomas (1991).

3 Determining Term Weights for Single Document Summarization

For SDS we consider three term weighting methods.

The first is global entropy as proposed by Dumais et al. for information retrieval (Dumais, 1994) (Rehder et al., 1997) and by Steinberger and Jezek for document summarization (Steinberger and Jezek, 2009). Global entropy weighting is given by

$$w_i^{(\mathrm{GE})} = 1 - \frac{\sum_j p_{i,j} \cdot \log p_{i,j}}{\log n},$$

where n is the number of sentences, $p_{i,j} = t_{ij}/f_i$, t_{ij} is the number of times term i appears in sentence j, and f_i is the total number of times term i appears in all sentences.[1]

The second term weighting is simply the logarithm of frequency of the term in all the sentences:

$$w_i^{(\mathrm{LF})} = 1 + \log(f_i).$$

Log frequency is motivated by the fact that the sum of the term scores for a given sentence is (up to an affine transformation) the log probability of generating that sentence by sampling terms independently at random, where the probability of each term is estimated by maximum likelihood from the observed frequencies f_i.

The third method is a personalized variant of TextRank, which was first proposed by Mihalcea (2005) and motivated by PageRank (Page et al., 1999). The personalized version smooths the Markov chain used in TextRank (PageRank) with term (page) preferences. Previously, a sentence based version of personalization has been used for summarization; see, for example, Zhao et al. (2009). Our current work may be the first use of a term based *personalized* TextRank (TermRank), which we call PTR. The personalization vector we choose is simply the normalized frequency, and the Markov chain is defined by the transition matrix

$$M = \frac{1}{2} L L^T D + \frac{1}{2} p e^T$$

where

$$p_i = f_i / \sum_i (f_i),$$

L is the incidence term-sentence matrix. The elements of L are previously defined local weights, ℓ_{ij}. The vector e is all 1's and D is a diagonal matrix chosen to make the column sums equal to one. The estimated weight vector used by OCCAMS_V, $w^{(\mathrm{PTR})}$, is computed using 5 iterations of the power method to approximate the stationary vector of this matrix. Note, there is no need to form the matrix M since the applications of M to a vector may be achieved by vector operations and matrix-vector multiplies by L and L^T.

We test the performance of these three term weighting methods on two data sets: DUC 2002 English single-document data and the Wikipedia Pilot at MultiLing 2013.

3.1 Results for DUC 2002 Data

The DUC 2002 English single-document data contains 567 newswire documents for which there are one or two human-generated summaries.

In addition to computing ROUGE-2 scores, we also compute an oracle coverage score (Conroy et al., 2006). At TAC 2011 (Conroy et al., 2011) (Rankel et al., 2012) bigram coverage was shown to be a useful feature for predicting the performance of automated summarization systems relative to a human summarizer. Oracle unigram coverage score is defined by

$$C_1(X) = \sum_{i \in T} f_1(i),$$

where T is the set of terms and $f_1(i)$ is the fraction of humans who included the ith term in the

[1] We make the usual convenient definition that $p_i \log p_i = 0$ when $p_i = 0$.

Term Weight	ROUGE-2	C_1	Group
PTR	0.194	19.1	1
LF	0.192	18.7	2
GE	0.190	18.6	2

Table 2: ROUGE-2 and Coverage bi-grams Scores

summary. More generally, we define C_n in similar way for n-gram oracle coverage scores. Coverage scores differ from ROUGE scores since the score is not affected by the number of times that a given human or machine-generated summary uses the term, but only whether or not the term is included in the machine summary and the estimated fraction of humans that would use this term. We note that this score can be modified to compute scores for human summarizers using the analogous jackknife procedure employed by ROUGE.

Table 2 gives a summary of the results. We ran a Wilcoxon test to check for statistical distinguishability in the performance of the different term-weighting methods. Methods were placed in the same group if they produced results in coverage (C_1) that were indistinguishable. More precisely, we used the null hypothesis that the difference between the vector of scores for two methods has median 0. If the p-value of two consecutive entries in the table was less than 0.05, the group label was increased and is shown in the last column.

Log frequency (LF) and global entropy (GE) are correlated. For the DUC 2002 data they perform comparably. Personalized term rank (PTR) weighting is statistically stronger than the other two approaches, as measured by the oracle term coverage score. For these data the definition of term for the purposes of the computation of the oracle coverage score is non-stop word stemmed (unigram) tokens.

3.2 Results for the Wikipedia Pilot at MultiLing 2013

This task involves single-document summarization for 1200 Wikipedia feature articles: 30 documents in each of 40 languages. For each document, the organizers generated a baseline lead summary consisting of the first portion of the feature article following the "hidden summary." Summary lengths were approximately 150 words for all non-ideograph languages and 500 characters for the ideograph languages. Sentences were ordered in the order selected by OCCAMS_V. Thus, sentences covering the largest number of relevant terms, as measured by the term-weighting scheme, will appear first.

Results of this pilot study will be presented in detail in the overview workshop paper, but we note here that, as measured by ROUGE-1, in 19 of the 40 languages, at least one of our three submitted methods significantly outperformed the lead-summary baseline.

4 Dimensionality Reduction

The goal of dimensionality reduction is to identify the major factors of the term-sentence matrix A and to throw away those factors which are "irrelevant" for summarization. Here we survey three algorithms: the well-known LSA, the more recent latent Dirichlet allocation (LDA), and the new interval-bounded nonnegative matrix factorization.

4.1 Latent Semantic Analysis

Davis et al. (2012) successfully used an approximation to A, computed using the singular value decomposition (SVD) $A = USV^T$. They used the first 200 columns U_{200} of the singular vector matrix U and the corresponding part of the singular value matrix S. They eliminated negative entries in U_{200} by taking absolute values. The term weights were computed as the L_1 norm (sum of the entries) in the rows of $W = |U_{200}|S_{200}$.

Our method is similar, except that we use 250 columns and form them in a slightly different way. Observe that in the SVD, if u_i is a column of U and v_i^T is a row of V, then they can be replaced by $-u_i$ and $-v_i^T$. This is true since if D is any diagonal matrix with entries $+1$ and -1, then

$$A = USV^T = (UD)S(DV^T).$$

Therefore, we propose choosing D so that the sum of the positive entries in each column of U is maximized. Then we form $\hat{U}$ by setting each negative entry of UD to zero and form $W = \hat{U}_{250}S_{250}$.

4.2 Latent Dirichlet Allocation

We use the term-sentence matrix to train a simple generative topic model based on LDA (Blei et al., 2003). This model is described by the following parameters: the number of terms m; the number of topics k; a vector w representing a probability distribution over topics; and an $m \times k$ matrix A in which each column represents a probability distribution over terms.

In this model, sentences are generated independently. We use the "pure-topic" LDA model and assume, for simplicity, that the length of the sentence is fixed *a priori*. First, a topic $i \in \{1, \ldots, k\}$ is chosen from the probability distribution w. Then, terms are generated by sampling independently from the distribution specified by the ith column of the matrix A.

We train this model using a recently-developed spectral algorithm based on third-order tensor decompositions (Anandkumar et al., 2012a; Anandkumar et al., 2012b). This algorithm is guaranteed to recover the parameters of the LDA model, provided that the columns of the matrix A are linearly independent. For our experiments, we used a Matlab implementation from Hsu (2012).

4.3 Interval Bounded Nonnegative Matrix Factorization (IBNMF)

We also use a new method for dimensionality reduction, a nonnegative matrix factorization algorithm that handles uncertainty in a new way (O'Leary and et al., In preparation).

Since the term-sentence matrix A is not known with certainty, let's suppose that we are given upper and lower bound matrices U and L so that $L \le A \le U$. We compute a sparse nonnegative low-rank approximation to A of the form XY, where X is nonnegative (i.e., $X \ge 0$) and has r columns and Y is nonnegative and has r rows. This gives us an approximate nonnegative factorization of A of rank at most r.

We choose to measure closeness of two matrices using the Frobenius norm-squared, where $\|Z\|_F^2$ denotes the sum of the squares of the entries of Z. Since A is sparse, we also want X and Y to be sparse. We use the common trick of forcing this by minimizing the sum of the entries of the matrices, denoted by $\text{sum}(X) + \text{sum}(Y)$. This leads us to determine X and Y by choosing a weighting constant α and solving

$$\min_{X,Y,Z} \quad \alpha \, \|XY - Z\|_F^2 + \text{sum}(X) + \text{sum}(Y)$$

subject to the constraints

$$\begin{aligned} L \le \; & Z \le U, \\ X & \ge 0, \\ Y & \ge 0. \end{aligned}$$

We simplify this problem by noting that for any $W = XY$, the entries of the optimal Z are

$$z_{ij} = \begin{cases} \ell_{ij}, & w_{ij} \le \ell_{ij}, \\ w_{ij}, & \ell_{ij} \le w_{ij} \le u_{ij}, \\ u_{ij}, & u_{ij} \le w_{ij}. \end{cases}$$

We solve our minimization problem by an alternating algorithm, iterating by fixing X and determining the optimal Y and then fixing Y and determining the optimal X. Either non-negativity is imposed during the solution to the subproblems, making each step more expensive, or negative entries of the updated matrices are set to zero, ruining theoretical convergence properties but yielding a more practical algorithm. Each iteration reduces the distance to the term matrix, but setting negative values to zero increases it again.

For our summarization system we chose $r = 50$ and $\alpha = 1000$. We scaled the rows of the matrix using global entropy weights and used $L = 0.9A$ and $U = 1.1A$.

4.4 Term Weighting and Dimension Choice for Multi-Document Summarization

A natural term weighting can be obtained by computing the row sums of the dimension-reduced approximation to the term-sentence matrix. For LSA, the resulting term weights are the sum of the entries in the rows of $W = \hat{U}_{250} S_{250}$. For the LDA method the initial matrix is the matrix of counts. The model has three components similar to that of the SVD in LSA, and the term weights are computed analogously. For IBNMF, the term weights are the sum of the entries in the rows of the optimal XY.

Each of the three dimensionality reduction methods require us to specify the dimension of the "topic space." We explored this question using the DUC 2005-2007 and the TAC 2011 data. Tables 3, 4, 5, and 6 give the average ROUGE-2, ROUGE-4, and bi-gram coverage scores, with confidence intervals, for the dimension that gave the best coverage. The optimal ranks were 250 for LSA, 5 for LDA, and 50 for IBNMF. We emphasize the these results are very strong despite the fact that no use of the topic descriptions or the guided summary aspects for the TAC 2010 and 2011 are used. Thus, we treat these data as if the task were to generate a generic summary, as is the case in the MultiLing 2013 task. [2]

[2]We note that some of the coverage (C_2), and ROUGE-

System	R_2	R_4	C_2
A	0.117 (0.106,0.129)	0.016 (0.011, 0.021)	26.333 (23.849,28.962)
C	0.118 (0.105,0.131)	0.016 (0.012, 0.022)	25.882 (23.086,28.710)
E	0.105 (0.092,0.120)	0.016 (0.010, 0.022)	23.625 (18.938,28.573)
F	0.100 (0.089,0.111)	0.014 (0.010, 0.019)	23.500 (19.319,27.806)
B	0.100 (0.086,0.115)	0.013 (0.008, 0.019)	23.118 (20.129,26.285)
D	0.100 (0.089,0.113)	0.012 (0.007, 0.017)	22.957 (20.387,25.742)
I	0.099 (0.085,0.116)	0.010 (0.007, 0.014)	21.806 (17.722,26.250)
H	0.088 (0.077,0.101)	0.011 (0.007, 0.016)	20.972 (17.389,24.750)
J	0.100 (0.090,0.111)	0.010 (0.007, 0.013)	20.472 (17.167,24.389)
G	0.097 (0.085,0.108)	0.012 (0.008, 0.017)	20.111 (16.694,24.000)
LSA250	0.085 (0.076,0.093)	0.008 (0.006, 0.009)	17.950 (17.072,18.838)
IBNMF50	0.079 (0.068,0.089)	0.007 (0.005, 0.009)	17.730 (16.843,18.614)
LDA5	0.077 (0.074,0.080)	0.008 (0.007, 0.009)	17.165 (16.320,18.024)

Table 3: DUC 2005

System	R_2	R_4	C_2
C	0.133 (0.116,0.152)	0.025 (0.018, 0.033)	30.517 (26.750,34.908)
D	0.124 (0.108,0.140)	0.017 (0.011, 0.023)	27.283 (23.567,31.050)
B	0.118 (0.105,0.134)	0.015 (0.012, 0.020)	25.933 (23.333,29.033)
G	0.113 (0.102,0.124)	0.016 (0.011, 0.022)	25.717 (23.342,28.017)
H	0.108 (0.098,0.117)	0.013 (0.010, 0.016)	24.767 (22.433,27.067)
F	0.109 (0.093,0.128)	0.016 (0.010, 0.023)	24.183 (20.650,28.292)
I	0.106 (0.096,0.116)	0.012 (0.008, 0.015)	24.133 (22.133,26.283)
J	0.107 (0.093,0.125)	0.015 (0.010, 0.022)	23.933 (20.908,27.233)
A	0.104 (0.093,0.116)	0.015 (0.010, 0.022)	23.283 (20.483,26.283)
E	0.104 (0.089,0.119)	0.014 (0.010, 0.020)	22.950 (19.833,26.450)
LDA5	0.103 (0.099,0.107)	0.012 (0.011, 0.013)	22.620 (21.772,23.450)
IBNMF50	0.095 (0.091,0.099)	0.010 (0.009, 0.011)	22.400 (21.615,23.177)
LSA250	0.099 (0.096,0.103)	0.012 (0.011, 0.013)	22.335 (21.497,23.200)

Table 4: DUC 2006

System	R_2	R_4	C_2
D	0.175 (0.157,0.196)	0.038 (0.029, 0.050)	39.481 (34.907,44.546)
C	0.151 (0.134,0.169)	0.035 (0.024, 0.049)	34.148 (29.870,38.926)
E	0.139 (0.125,0.154)	0.025 (0.020, 0.030)	30.907 (27.426,34.574)
J	0.139 (0.120,0.160)	0.028 (0.019, 0.038)	30.759 (25.593,36.389)
B	0.140 (0.116,0.163)	0.027 (0.019, 0.036)	30.537 (25.815,35.537)
I	0.136 (0.113,0.159)	0.022 (0.014, 0.030)	30.537 (25.806,35.241)
G	0.134 (0.118,0.150)	0.027 (0.018, 0.035)	30.259 (26.509,33.926)
F	0.134 (0.120,0.149)	0.024 (0.017, 0.033)	29.944 (26.481,33.870)
A	0.133 (0.117,0.149)	0.024 (0.016, 0.033)	29.315 (25.685,33.093)
H	0.130 (0.117,0.143)	0.020 (0.015, 0.027)	28.815 (25.537,32.185)
IBNMF50	0.140 (0.122,0.158)	0.023 (0.017, 0.031)	28.350 (27.092,29.567)
LSA250	0.125 (0.120,0.130)	0.022 (0.020, 0.024)	28.144 (26.893,29.344)
LDA5	0.124 (0.118,0.129)	0.021 (0.019, 0.023)	27.722 (26.556,28.893)

Table 5: DUC 2007

System	R_2	R_4	C_2
IBNMF50	0.132 (0.124,0.140)	0.033 (0.029, 0.038)	12.585 (11.806,13.402)
D	0.128 (0.110,0.146)	0.024 (0.017, 0.032)	12.212 (10.394,14.045)
LSA250	0.128 (0.120,0.136)	0.030 (0.025, 0.034)	12.210 (11.441,12.975)
A	0.119 (0.099,0.138)	0.024 (0.016, 0.033)	11.591 (9.758,13.455)
LDA5	0.120 (0.112,0.128)	0.028 (0.024, 0.033)	11.409 (10.678,12.159)
E	0.118 (0.099,0.138)	0.025 (0.016, 0.035)	11.288 (9.409,13.258)
H	0.115 (0.097,0.132)	0.020 (0.014, 0.027)	11.212 (9.439,12.955)
B	0.111 (0.099,0.125)	0.018 (0.013, 0.023)	10.591 (9.379,11.864)
F	0.109 (0.090,0.128)	0.017 (0.010, 0.025)	10.530 (8.515,12.500)
C	0.110 (0.095,0.126)	0.015 (0.010, 0.021)	10.379 (8.939,11.924)
G	0.110 (0.092,0.127)	0.016 (0.010, 0.023)	10.258 (8.682,11.894)

Table 6: TAC 2011

5 Sentence Selection

Our sentence selection algorithm, OCCAMS_V, is an extension of the one used in (Davis et al., 2012), which uses the $(1 - e^{-1/2})$-approximation scheme for the Budgeted Maximal Coverage (BMC) problem and the Dynamic Programming based FPTAS for the knapsack problem.

Algorithm **OCCAMS_V** (T, $\mathcal{D}, \mathcal{W}, c, L$)
1. K_1 = Greedy_BMC($T, \mathcal{D}, \mathcal{W}, c, L$)
2. $K_2 = S_{max} \cup$ Greedy_BMC($T', \mathcal{D}', \mathcal{W}, c', L'$)), where $S_{max} = \text{argmax}_{\{S_i \in \mathcal{D}\}}\left\{ \sum_{t_j \in S_i} w(t_j)\right\}$ and $T', \mathcal{D}', \mathcal{W}, c', L'$ represent quantities updated by deleting sentence S_{max} from the collection.
3. K_3 = KS(Greedy_BMC($T, \mathcal{D}, \mathcal{W}, c, 5L$), L);
4. K_4 = KS(K_4', L), where $K_4' = S_{max} \cup$ Greedy_BMC($T', \mathcal{D}', \mathcal{W}, \mathcal{C}', 5L'$));
5. $K = \text{argmax}_{k=1,2,3,4}\left\{ \sum_{T(K_i)} w(t_i)\right\}$ where $T(K_i)$ is the set of terms covered by K_i.

This algorithm selects minimally overlapping sentences, thus reducing redundancy, while maximizing term coverage. The algorithm guarantees a $(1 - e^{-1/2})$ approximation ratio for BMC.

We use the m terms $T = \{t_1, \ldots, t_m\}$ and their corresponding weights $\mathcal{W} = \{w_1, \ldots, w_m\}$. We also use the n sentences $\mathcal{D} = \{S_1, \ldots, S_n\}$, where each S_i is the set of terms in the ith sentence, so that $S_i \subseteq T$. We define c to be a vector whose components are the lengths of each sentence. Our algorithm, OCCAMS_V, determines four candidate sets of summary sentences and then chooses the one with maximal coverage weight. The first three candidate sets were used in the OCCAMS algorithm (Davis et al., 2012). The set K_1 is determined using the Greedy_BMC heuristic of Khuller et al. (1999) to maximize the sum of weights corresponding to terms in the summary sentences. The set K_2 is determined the same way, but the sentence that has the best sum of weights is forced to be included. The third candidate K_3 is determined by applying a fully polynomial-time approximation scheme (FPTAS) dynamic programming algorithm, denoted by KS, to the knapsack problem using sentences chosen by the Greedy_BMC heuristic, asking for a length of $5L$. The fourth candidate K_4 is similar, but the sentence with the best sum of weights is forced to be included in the input to KS.

OCCAMS_V guarantees an approximation ratio of $(1 - e^{-1/2})$ for the result because the quality of the solution chosen is no worse than the approximation ratio achieved by the OCCAMS algorithm.

2 scores reported in (Davis et al., 2012), where a rank 200 approximation and a large background corpus were used, are higher than the ones reported here, where a small self-background and a rank 250 approximation is used.

6 Coverage Results for MultiLing 2013

We defined a term oracle coverage score in Section 3.1, an automatic summarization evaluation score that computes the expected number of n-grams that a summary will have in common with a human summary selected at random, assuming that humans select terms independently. As reported in (Davis et al., 2012), the 2-gram oracle coverage correlates as well with human evaluations of English summaries as ROUGE-2 does for English newswire summaries.[3] It is natural then to ask to what extent oracle coverage scores can predict a summary's quality for other languages.

[3]Here a term is defined as a stemmed 2-gram token.

For each of the 10 MultiLing 2013 languages we can tokenize and generate bigrams (or character n-grams for Chinese) for the human-generated summaries and the machine-generated summaries. Table 7 gives the average oracle term (bi-gram) coverage score (C_2) for the lowest-scoring human and for each of the dimensionality reduction algorithms described in Section 4.

In all but four of the languages (Romanian, Hindi, Spanish, and Chinese), at least one of our methods scored higher than the lowest scoring human. As with the DUC and TAC testing, the LDA method of term-weighting was the weakest of the three. In fact, in eight of the languages one or both of OCCAMS_V(LSA) and OCCAMS_V(IBNMF) (indicated in boldface in the table) scored significantly higher than OCCAMS_V(LDA) (p-value < 0.05 using a paired Wilcoxon test).

The human coverage scores for three of the languages (Romanian, Hindi, and Chinese) are surprisingly high. Examining these data more closely indicates that a large number of the summaries are nearly identical. As an example, in one of the Romanian document sets, there were 266 bi-grams in the union of the three summaries, and the summary length was 250. Document sets similar to this are the major cause of the anomalously high scores for humans in these languages.

Language	Human	LSA	IBNMF	LDA
english	37	**38**	**37**	34
arabic	22	**29**	**28**	23
czech	22	34	35	33
french	28	**38**	**38**	34
greek	19	25	**25**	24
hebrew	16	19	**22**	19
hindi	64	**20**	20	18
spanish	47	**40**	**44**	36
romanian	118	31	28	29
chinese	68	**23**	**24**	18

Table 7: MultiLing 2013 Coverage Results

Human evaluation of the multi-lingual multi-document summaries is currently under way. These evaluations will be extremely informative and will help measure to what extent ROUGE, coverage, and character n-gram based methods such as MeMoG (Giannakopoulos et al., 2010), are effective in predicting performance.

7 Conclusions and Future Work

In this paper we presented three term weighting approaches for single document multi-lingual summarization. These approaches were tested on the DUC 2002 data and on a submission to the MultiLing 2013 single document pilot task for all 40 languages. Automatic evaluation of these summaries with ROUGE-1 indicates that the strongest of the approaches significantly outperformed the lead baseline. The Wikipedia feature articles pose a challenge due to their variable summary size and genre. Further analysis of the results as well as human evaluation of the submitted summaries would deepen our understanding.

A new nonnegative matrix factorization method, interval bounded nonnegative matrix factorization (IBNMF), was used. This method allows specifying interval bounds, which give an intuitive way to express uncertainty in the term-sentence matrix.

For MDS we presented a variation of a LSA term-weighting for OCCAMS_V as well as novel use of both of the IBNMF and an LDA model.

Based on automatic evaluation using coverage, it appears that the LSA method and the IBNMF term-weighting give rise to competitive summaries with term coverage scores approaching that of humans for 6 of the 10 languages. The automatic evaluation of these summaries, which should soon be finished, will be illuminating.

References

Anima Anandkumar, Dean P. Foster, Daniel Hsu, Sham Kakade, and Yi-Kai Liu. 2012a. A spectral algorithm for latent dirichlet allocation. In Peter L. Bartlett, Fernando C. N. Pereira, Christopher J. C. Burges, Léon Bottou, and Kilian Q. Weinberger, editors, *NIPS*, pages 926–934.

Anima Anandkumar, Rong Ge, Daniel Hsu, Sham M. Kakade, and Matus Telgarsky. 2012b. Tensor decompositions for learning latent variable models. *CoRR*, abs/1210.7559.

David M. Blei, Andrew Y. Ng, and Michael I. Jordan. 2003. Latent dirichlet allocation. *Journal of Machine Learning Research*, 3:993–1022.

John M. Conroy, Judith D. Schlesinger, and Dianne P. O'Leary. 2006. Topic-focused multi-document summarization using an approximate oracle score. In *Proceedings of the ACL'06/COLING'06 Conferences*, pages 152–159, Sydney, Australia, July.

John M Conroy, Judith D Schlesinger, and Dianne P O'leary. 2009. Classy 2009: summarization and metrics. *Proceedings of the text analysis conference (TAC)*.

John M Conroy, Judith D Schlesinger, Jeff Kubina, Peter A Rankel, and Dianne P O'Leary. 2011. Classy 2011 at tac: Guided and multi-lingual summaries and evaluation metrics. *Proceedings of the Text Analysis Conference*.

Thomas M. Cover and Joy A. Thomas. 1991. *Elements of information theory*. Wiley-Interscience, New York, NY, USA.

Sashka T. Davis, John M. Conroy, and Judith D. Schlesinger. 2012. Occams - an optimal combinatorial covering algorithm for multi-document summarization. In Jilles Vreeken, Charles Ling, Mohammed Javeed Zaki, Arno Siebes, Jeffrey Xu Yu, Bart Goethals, Geoffrey I. Webb, and Xindong Wu, editors, *ICDM Workshops*, pages 454–463. IEEE Computer Society.

Susan T. Dumais. 1994. Latent semantic indexing (lsi): Trec-3 report. In *TREC*, pages 105–115.

Ted Dunning. 1993. Accurate methods for the statistics of surprise and coincidence. *Computational Linguistics*, 19(1):61–74.

George Giannakopoulos, George A. Vouros, and Vangelis Karkaletsis. 2010. Mudos-ng: Multi-document summaries using n-gram graphs (tech report). *CoRR*, abs/1012.2042.

Daniel Hsu. 2012. Estimating a simple topic model. `http://cseweb.ucsd.edu/~djhsu/code/learn_topics.m`.

Samir Khuller, Anna Moss, and Joseph Naor. 1999. The Budgeted Maximum Coverage Problem. *Inf. Process. Lett.*, 70(1):39–45.

Chin-Yew Lin and Eduard Hovy. 2000. The automated acquisition of topic signatures for text summarization. In *Proceedings of the 18th conference on Computational linguistics*, pages 495–501, Morristown, NJ, USA. Association for Computational Linguistics.

Rada Mihalcea. 2005. Language independent extractive summarization. In *Proceedings of ACL 2005*, Ann Arbor, MI, USA.

Dianne P. O'Leary and et al. In preparation. An interval bounded nonnegative matrix factorization. Technical report.

Lawrence Page, Sergey Brin, Rajeev Motwani, and Terry Winograd. 1999. The pagerank citation ranking: Bringing order to the web. Technical Report 1999-66, Stanford InfoLab, November. Previous number = SIDL-WP-1999-0120.

Peter A. Rankel, John M. Conroy, and Judith D. Schlesinger. 2012. Better metrics to automatically predict the quality of a text summary. *Algorithms*, 5(4):398–420.

Bob Rehder, Michael L. Littman, Susan T. Dumais, and Thomas K. Landauer. 1997. Automatic 3-language cross-language information retrieval with latent semantic indexing. In *TREC*, pages 233–239.

Gerard Salton. 1991. The smart information retrieval system after 30 years - panel. In Abraham Bookstein, Yves Chiaramella, Gerard Salton, and Vijay V. Raghavan, editors, *SIGIR*, pages 356–358. ACM.

Josef Steinberger and Karel Jezek. 2009. Update summarization based on novel topic distribution. In *ACM Symposium on Document Engineering*, pages 205–213.

Lin Zhao, Lide Wu, and Xuanjing Huang. 2009. Using query expansion in graph-based approach for query-focused multi-document summarization. *Information Processing & Management*, 45(1):35 – 41.

Using a Keyness Metric for Single and Multi Document Summarisation

Mahmoud El-Haj
School of Computing and Communications
Lancaster University
United Kingdom
m.el-haj@lancaster.ac.uk

Paul Rayson
School of Computing and Communications
Lancaster University
United Kingdom
p.rayson@lancaster.ac.uk

Abstract

In this paper we show the results of our participation in the MultiLing 2013 summarisation tasks. We participated with single-document and multi-document corpus-based summarisers for both Arabic and English languages. The summarisers used word frequency lists and log likelihood calculations to generate single and multi document summaries. The single and multi summaries generated by our systems were evaluated by Arabic and English native speaker participants and by different automatic evaluation metrics, ROUGE, AutoSummENG, MeMoG and NPowER. We compare our results to other systems that participated in the same tracks on both Arabic and English languages. Our single-document summarisers performed particularly well in the automatic evaluation with our English single-document summariser performing better on average than the results of the other participants. Our Arabic multi-document summariser performed well in the human evaluation ranking second.

1 Introduction

Systems that can automatically summarise documents are becoming ever more desirable with the increasing volume of information available on the Web. Automatic text summarisation is the process of producing a shortened version of a text by the use of computers. For example, reducing a text document or a group of related documents into a shorter version of sentences or paragraphs using automated tools and techniques.

The summary should convey the key contributions of the text. In other words, only key sentences should appear in the summary and the process of defining those sentences is highly dependent on the summarisation method used. In automatic summarisation there are two main approaches that are broadly used, extractive and abstractive. The first method, the extractive summarisation, extracts, up to a certain limit, the key sentences or paragraphs from the text and orders them in a way that will produce a coherent summary. The extracted units differ from one summariser to another. Most summarisers use sentences rather than larger units such as paragraphs. Extractive summarisation methods are the focus method on automatic text summarisation. The other method, abstractive summarisation, involves more language dependent tools and Natural Language Generation (NLG) technology. In our work we used extractive single and multi-document Arabic and English summarisers.

A successful summarisation approach needs a good guide to find the most important sentences that are relevant to a certain criterion. Therefore, the proposed methods should work on extracting the most important sentences from a set of related articles.

In this paper we present the results of our participation to the MultiLing 2013 summarisation tasks. MultiLing 2013 was built upon the Text Analysis Conference (TAC) MultiLing Pilot task of 2011 (Giannakopoulos et al., 2011). MultiLing 2013 this year asked for participants to run their summarisers on different languages having a corpus and gold standard summaries in the same seven languages (Arabic, Czech, English, French, Greek, Hebrew or Hindi) of TAC 2011 with a 50% increase to the corpora size. It also introduced three new languages (Chinese, Romanian and Spanish). MultiLing 2013 this year introduced a new single-document summarisation pilot for 40 languages including the above mentioned languages (in our case Arabic and English).

In this paper we introduce the results of our

single-document and multi-document summarisers at the MultiLing 2013 summarisation tasks. We used a language independent corpus-based word frequency technique and the log-likelihood statistic to extract sentences with the maximum sum of log likelihood. The output summary is expected to be no more than 250 words.

2 Related Work

2.1 Automatic Summarisation

Work on automatic summarisation dates back more than 50 years, with a focus on the English language (Luhn, 1958). The work on Arabic automatic summarisation is more recent and still not on par with the research on English and other European languages. Early work on Arabic summarisation started less than 10 years ago (Conroy et al., 2006; Douzidia and Lapalme, 2004).

Over time, there have been various approaches to automatic text summarisation. These approaches include single-document and multi-document summarisation. Both single-document and multi-document summarisation use the summarisation methods mentioned earlier, i.e. extractive or abstractive. Summarising a text could be dependent on input information such as a user query or it could be generic where no user query is used.

The approach of single-document summarisation relies on the idea of producing a summary for a single document. The main factor in single-document summarisation is to identify the most important (informative) parts of a document. Early work on single-document summarisation was the work by Luhn (1958). In his work he looked for sentences containing keywords that are most frequent in a text. The sentences with highly weighted keywords were selected. The work by Luhn highlighted the need for features that reflect the importance of a certain sentence in a text. Baxendale (1958) showed the importance of sentence-position in a text, which is understood to be one of the earliest extracted features in automatic text summarisation. They took a sample of 200 paragraphs and found that in 80% of the paragraphs the most important sentence was the first one.

Multi-document summarisation produces a single summary of a set of documents. The documents are assumed to be about the same genre and topic. The analysis in this area is performed typically at either the sentence or document level.

2.2 Corpus-based and Word Frequency in Summarisation

Corpus-based techniques are mainly used to compare corpora for linguistic analysis (Rayson and Garside, 2000; Rayson et al., 2004). There are two main types of corpora comparisons, 1) comparing a sample corpus with a larger standard corpus (Scott, 2000). 2) comparing two corpora of equal size (Granger, 1998). In our work we adopted the first approach, where we used a much larger reference corpus. The first word list is the frequency list of all the words in the document (or group of documents) to be summarised which is compared to the word frequency list of a much larger standard corpus. We do that for both Arabic and English texts. Word frequency has been proven as an important feature when determining a sentence's importance (Li et al., 2006). Nenkova and Vanderwende (2005) studies the impact of frequency on summarisation. In their work they investigated the association between words that appear frequently in a document (group of related documents), and the likelihood that they will be selected by a human summariser to be included in a summary. Taking the top performing summarisers at the DUC 2003[1] they computed how many of the top frequency words from the input documents appeared in the system summaries. They found the following: 1) Words with high frequency in the input documents are very likely to appear in the human summaries. 2) The automatic summarisers include less of these high frequency words. These two findings by Nenkova and Vanderwende (2005) tell us two important facts. Firstly, it confirms that word frequency is an important factor that impacts humans' decisions on which content to include in the summary. Secondly, the overlap between human and system summaries can be improved by including more of the high frequency words in the generated system summaries. Based on Nenkova's study we expand the work on word frequency by comparing word frequency lists of different corpora in a way to select sentences with the maximum sum of log likelihood ratio. The log-likelihood calculation favours words whose frequencies are unexpectedly high in a document.

2.3 Statistical Summarisation

The use of statistical approaches (e.g. log-likelihood) in text summarisation is a common

[1] http://duc.nist.gov/duc2003/tasks.html

technique, especially when building a language independent text summariser.

Morita et al. (2011) introduced what they called "query-snowball", a method for query-oriented extractive multi-document summarisation. They worked on closing the gap between the query and the relevant sentences. They formulated the summarisation problem based on word pairs as a maximum cover problem with Knapsack Constraints (MCKP), which is an optimisation problem that maximises the total score of words covered by a summary within a certain length limit.

Knight and Marcu (2000) used the Expectation Maximisation (EM) algorithm to compress sentences for an abstractive text summarisation system. EM is an iterative method for finding Maximum Likelihood (ML) or Maximum A Posteriori (MAP) estimates of parameters in statistical models. In their summariser, EM was used in the sentences compression process to shorten many sentences into one by compressing a syntactic parse tree of a sentence in order to produce a shorter but maximally grammatical version. Similarly, Madnani et al. (2007) performed multi-document summarisation by generating compressed versions of source sentences as summary candidates and used weighted features of these candidates to construct summaries.

Hennig (2009) introduced a query-based latent Semantic Analysis (LSA) automatic text summariser. It finds statistical semantic relationships between the extracted sentences rather than word by word matching relations (Hofmann, 1999). The summariser selects sentences with the highest likelihood score.

In our work we used log-likelihood to select sentences with the maximum sum of log likelihood scores, unlike the traditional method of measuring cosine similarity overlap between articles or sentences to indicate importance (Luhn, 1958; Barzilay et al., 2001; Radev et al., 2004). The main advantage of our approach is that the automatic summariser does not need to compare sentences in a document with an initial one (e.g. first sentence or a query). Our approach works by calculating the keyness (or log-likelihood) score for each token (word) in a sentence, then picks, to a limit of 250 words, the sentences with the highest sum of the tokens' log-likelihood scores.

To the best of our knowledge the use of corpus-based frequency list to calculate the log-likelihood score for text summarisation has not been reported for the Arabic language.

3 Dataset and Evaluation Metrics

3.1 Test Collection

The test collection for the MultiLing 2013 is available in the previously mentioned languages.[2] The dataset is based on WikiNews texts.[3] The source documents contain no meta-data or tags and are represented as UTF8 plain text les. The multi-document dataset of each language contains (100-150) articles divided into 10 or 15 reference sets, each contains 10 related articles discussing the same topic. The original language of the dataset is English. The organisers of the tasks were responsible for translating the corpus into different languages by having native speaker participants for each of the 10 languages. In addition to the news articles the dataset also provides human-generated multi-document gold standard summaries. The single-document dataset contains single documents for 40 language (30 documents each) discussing various topics and collected from Wikipedia.[4]

3.2 Evaluation

Evaluating the quality and consistency of a generated summary has proven to be a difficult problem (Fiszman et al., 2009). This is mainly because there is no obvious ideal, objective summary. Two classes of metrics have been developed: form metrics and content metrics. Form metrics focus on grammaticality, overall text coherence, and organisation. They are usually measured on a point scale (Brandow et al., 1995). Content metrics are more difficult to measure. Typically, system output is compared sentence by sentence or unit by unit to one or more human-generated ideal summaries. As with information retrieval, the percentage of information presented in the system's summary (precision) and the percentage of important information omitted from the summary (recall) can be assessed. There are various models for system evaluation that may help in solving this problem. This include automatic evaluations (e.g. ROUGE and AutoSummENG), and human-performed evaluations. For the MultiLing 2013 task, the summaries generated by the participants

[2]http://multiling.iit.demokritos.gr/file/all
[3]http://www.wikinews.org/
[4]http://www.wikipedia.org/

were evaluated automatically based on human-generated model summaries provided by fluent speakers of each corresponding language (native speakers in the general case). The models used were, ROUGE variations (ROUGE1, ROUGE2, ROUGE-SU4) (Lin, 2004), the MeMoG variation (Giannakopoulos and Karkaletsis, 2011) of AutoSummENG (Giannakopoulos et al., 2008) and NPowER (Giannakopoulos and Karkaletsis, 2013). ROUGE was not used to evaluate the single-document summaries.

The summaries were also evaluated manually by human participants. For the manual evaluation the human evaluators were provided with the following guidelines: Each summary is to be assigned an integer grade from 1 to 5, related to the overall responsiveness of the summary. We consider a text to be worth a 5, if it appears to cover all the important aspects of the corresponding document set using fluent, readable language. A text should be assigned a 1, if it is either unreadable, nonsensical, or contains only trivial information from the document set. We consider the content and the quality of the language to be equally important in the grading.

Note, the human evaluation results for the English language are not included in this paper as by the time of writing the results were not yet published. We only report the human evaluation results of the Arabic multi-document summaries.

4 Corpus-based Summarisation

Our summarisation approach is a corpus-based where we use word frequency lists to compare corpora and calculate the log likelihood score for each word in the list. The compared corpora include standard Arabic and English corpora in addition to the Arabic and English summarisation datasets provided by MultiLing 2013 for the single and multi-document summarisation tasks. The subsections below describe the creation of the word lists and the standard corpora we used for the comparison process.

4.1 Word Frequencies

We used a simple methodology to generate the word frequency lists for the Arabic and English summarisation datasets provided by MultiLing 2013. The datasets used in our experiments were single-document and multi-document documents in English and Arabic. For the multi-document

word	frequency
المتحدة	33
ان	32
ايران	31
تم	29
قبل	25
المملكة	25
كان	24
البريطانية	24
ومشاة	19
البريطانيين	19

(a) Arabic Sample

word	frequency
government	21
personnel	21
release	20
Royal	17
would	17
this	16
into	16
United	15
Iraq	14
UK	14

(b) English Sample

Figure 1: Arabic and English Word Frequency List Sample

dataset we counted the word frequency for all the documents in a reference set (group of related articles), each set contains on average 10 related articles. The single-document dataset was straightforward, we calculated word frequencies for all the words in each document. Figure 1 shows a sample of random words and their frequencies for both Arabic and English languages. The sample was selected from the MultiLing dataset word frequency lists. As shown in the figure we did not eliminate the stop-words, we treat them as normal words.

4.2 Standard Corpora

In our work we compared the word frequency list of the summarisation dataset against the larger Arabic and English standard corpora. For each of the standard corpora we had a list of word frequencies (up to 5,000 words) for both Arabic and English using the frequency dictionary of Arabic (Buckwalter and Parkinson, 2011) and the Corpus of Contemporary American English (COCA) top 5,000 words (Davies, 2010).

The frequency dictionary of Arabic provides a list of the 5,000 most frequently used words in Modern Standard Arabic (MSA) in addition to several of the most widely spoken Arabic dialects. The list was created based on a 30-million-word corpus of Arabic including written and spoken material from all around the Arab world. The Arabic summarisation dataset provided by MultiLing 2013 was also written using MSA. The corpus of contemporary American English COCA is a freely searchable 450-million-word corpus containing text in American English of different number of genres. To be consistent with the Arabic word frequency list, we used the top 5000 words from the 450 million word COCA corpus.

5 Summarisation Methodology

In our experiments we used generic single-document and multi-document extractive summarisers that have been implemented for both Arabic and English (using identical processing pipelines for both languages). Summaries were created by selecting sentences from a single document or set of related documents. The following subsections show the methods used in our experiments, the actual summarisation process and the experimental setup.

5.1 Calculating Log-Likelihood

We begin the summarisation process by calculating the log likelihood score for each word in the word frequency lists (see Section 4.1) using the same methodology described in (Rayson and Garside, 2000). This was performed by constructing a contingency table as in Table 1.

	Corpus One	Corpus Two	Total
Frequency of Word	a	b	a+b
Frequency of other words	c-a	d-b	c+d-a-b
Total	c	d	c+d

Table 1: Contingency Table

The values c and d correspond to the number of words in corpus one and corpus two respectively. Where a and b are the observed values (O). For each corpus we calculated the expected value E using the following formula:

$$E_i = \frac{N_i \sum_i O_i}{\sum_i N_i}$$

N_i is the total frequency in corpus i (i in our case takes the values 1 (c) and 2 (d) for the MultiLing Arabic Summaries dataset and the frequency dictionary of Arabic (or MultiLing English Summaries dataset and COCA corpus) respectively.

The log-likelihood can be calculated as follows:

$$LL = 2 * ((a * \ln(\frac{a}{E1})) + (b * \ln(\frac{b}{E2})))$$

5.2 Summarisation Process

We used the same processing pipeline for both the single-document and multi-document summarisers. For each word in the MultiLing summarisation dataset (Arabic and English) we calculated the log likelihood scores using the calculations described in Section 5.1. We summed up the log likelihood scores for each sentence in the dataset and we picked the sentences (up to 250 word limit) with the highest sum of log likelihood scores. The main difference between the single-document and multi-document summarisers is that we treat the set of related documents in the multiling dataset as one document.

6 Single-Document Summarisation Task

MultiLing 2013 this year introduced a new single-document summarisation pilot for 40 languages including (Arabic, Czech, English, French, Greek, Hebrew, Hindi, Spanish, Chinese, Romanian ...etc). In our case we participated in two languages only, English and Arabic.

The pilot aim was to measure the ability of automated systems to apply single document summarisation, in the context of Wikipedia texts. Given a single encyclopedic entry, with several sections/subsections, describing a specific subject, the pilot guidelines asked the participating systems to provide a summary covering the main points of the entry (similarly to the lead section of a Wikipedia page). The MultiLing 2013 single-document summaries dataset consisted of (non-parallel) documents in the above mentioned languages.

For the English language, there were 7 participants (peers) including a baseline system ($ID5$). The Arabic language had 6 participants including the same baseline system.

7 Multi-Document Summarisation Task

The Multi-document summarisation task required the participants to generate a single, fluent, representative summary from a set of documents describing an event sequence. The language of the document set was within a given range of languages and all documents in a set shared the same language. The task guidelines required the output summary to be of the same language as its source documents. The output summary should be 250 words at most.

The set of documents were available in 10 languages (Arabic, Czech, English, French, Greek, Hebrew, Hindi, Spanish, Chinese and Romanian). In our case we participated using the Arabic and English set of documents only.

For the English language, there were 10 participants (peers) including a baseline ($ID6$) and a topline ($ID61$) systems. The Arabic language had 10 participants as well, including the same baseline and topline systems.

The baseline summariser sorted sentences based on their cosine similarity to the centroid of a cluster. Then starts adding sentences to the summary, until it either reaches 250 words, or it hits the end of the document. In the second case, it continues with the next document in the sorted list.

The topline summariser used information from the model summaries (i.e. cheats). First, it split all source documents into sentences. Then it used a genetic algorithm to generate summaries that have a vector with maximal cosine similarity to the centroid vector of the model summary texts.

8 Results and Discussion

Our single-document summarisers, both English and Arabic, performed particularly well in the automatic evaluation. Ranking first and second respectively.

Tables 2 and 3 illustrate the AutoSummEng (AutoSumm), MeMoG and NPowER results and the ranking of our English and Arabic single-document summarisers (System **ID2**).

System	AutoSumm	MeMoG	NPowER
ID2	0.136	0.136	1.685
ID41	0.129	0.129	1.661
ID42	0.127	0.127	1.656
ID3	0.127	0.127	1.654
ID1	0.124	0.124	1.647
ID4	0.123	0.123	1.641
ID5	0.040	0.040	1.367

Table 2: English Automatic Evaluation Scores (single-document)

The evaluation scores of our single-document summarisers confirm with (Li et al., 2006) and (Nenkova and Vanderwende, 2005) findings, were they found that word frequency is an important feature when determining sentences importance and that words with high frequency in the input documents are very likely to appear in the human summaries, which explains the high correlation between our single-document and the human (model) summaries as illustrated in the evaluation scores (Tables 2 and 3). The single-document summaries were evaluated automatically only.

System	AutoSumm	MeMoG	NPowER
ID3	0.092	0.092	1.538
ID2	0.087	0.087	1.524
ID41	0.055	0.055	1.418
ID42	0.055	0.055	1.416
ID4	0.053	0.053	1.411
ID5	0.025	0.025	1.317

Table 3: Arabic Automatic Evaluation Scores (single-document)

System	Score
ID6	3.711
ID3	3.578
ID2	3.578
ID4	3.489
ID1	3.467
ID11	3.333
ID21	3.111
ID51	2.778
ID5	2.711
ID61	2.489

Table 4: Arabic Manual Evaluation Scores (multi-document)

Our Arabic multi-document summariser performed well in the human evaluation ranking second jointly with System ID2. Table 4 shows the average scores of the human evaluation process, our system is referred to as **ID3**. On the other hand, we did not perform well in the automatic evaluation of the multi-document summarisation task for both English and Arabic. Our systems did not perform better than the baseline. The automatic evaluation results placed our Arabic and English summariser further down in the ranked lists of systems compared to the human assessment. This is an area for future work as this seems to suggest that the automatic evaluation metrics are not necessarily in line with human judgements.

The low automatic evaluation scores are due to two main reasons. First, we treated the set of related documents (multi-documents) as a single big document (See Section 5.2), this penalised our summaries as selecting the sentences with the maximum sum of log likelihood score lead to many important sentences being overlooked. This can be solved by running the summariser on each document to suggest candidate sentences and then selecting the top sentence(s) of each document to generate the final summary. Second, we did not work on eliminating redundancies. Finally, the log-likelihood score might be improved by the inclusion of a dispersion score or weighting to examine the evenness of the spread of each word across all the documents.

9 Conclusion

In this paper we presented the results of our participation in the MultiLing 2013 summarisation task. We submitted results for single-document and multi-document summarisation in two languages, English and Arabic. We applied a corpus-based summariser that used corpus-based word frequency lists. We used a list of the 5,000 most frequently used words in Modern Standard Arabic (MSA) and English. Using the frequency dictionary of Arabic and the corpus of contemporary American English (COCA).

Based on the automatic evaluation scores, we found that our approach appears to work very well for Arabic and English single-document summarisation. According to the human evaluation scores the approach could potentially work for Arabic multi-document summarisation as well. We believe that the approach could still work well for multi-document summarisation following the suggested solutions in Section 8.

References

R. Barzilay, N. Elhadad, and K. McKeown. 2001. Sentence Ordering in Multidocument Summarization. In *Proceedings of the First International Conference on Human Language Technology Research*, HLT'01, pages 1–7, Stroudsburg, PA, USA. Association for Computational Linguistics.

P. Baxendale. 1958. Machine-made index for technical literature: an experiment. *IBM Journal of Research and Development*, 2(4):354–361.

R. Brandow, K. Mitze, and Lisa F. Rau. 1995. Automatic Condensation of Electronic Publications by Sentence Selection. *Inf. Process. Manage.*, 31(5):675–685.

T. Buckwalter and D. Parkinson. 2011. *A Frequency Dictionary of Arabic: Core Vocabulary for Learners*. Routledge, London, United Kingdom.

J. Conroy, J. Schlesinger, D. O'Leary, and J. Goldstein. 2006. Back to Basics: CLASSY 2006. In *Proceedings of the 6th Document Understanding Conferences*. DUC.

M. Davies. 2010. The Corpus of Contemporary American English as the First Reliable Monitor Corpus of English. *Literary and Linguistic Computing*, 25:447–464.

F. Douzidia and G. Lapalme. 2004. Lakhas, an Arabic Summarising System. In *Proceedings of the 4th Document Understanding Conferences* , pages 128–135. DUC.

M. Fiszman, D. Demner-Fushman, H. Kilicoglu, and T. Rindflesch. 2009. Automatic Summarization of MEDLINE Citations for Evidence-based Medical Treatment: A Topic-oriented Evaluation. *Jouranl of Biomedical Informatics*, 42(5):801–813.

G. Giannakopoulos and V. Karkaletsis. 2011. AutoSummENG and MeMoG in Evaluating Guided Summaries. In *The Proceedings of the Text Analysis Conference*, MD, USA. TAC.

G. Giannakopoulos and V. Karkaletsis. 2013. Summary evaluation: Together we stand npower-ed. In Alexander Gelbukh, editor, *Computational Linguistics and Intelligent Text Processing*, volume 7817 of *Lecture Notes in Computer Science*, pages 436–450. Springer Berlin Heidelberg.

G. Giannakopoulos, V. Karkaletsis, G. Vouros, and P. Stamatopoulos. 2008. Summarization System Evaluation Revisited: N–Gram Graphs. *ACM Transactions on Speech and Language Processing (TSLP)*, 5(3):1–39.

G. Giannakopoulos, M. El-Haj, B. Favre, M. Litvak, J. Steinberger, and V. Varma. 2011. TAC 2011 MultiLing Pilot Overview. In *Text Analysis Conference (TAC) 2011, MultiLing Summarisation Pilot*, Maryland, USA. TAC.

S. Granger. 1998. The computer learner corpus: A versatile new source of data for SLA research. pages 3–18.

L. Hennig. 2009. Topic-based multi-document summarization with probabilistic latent semantic analysis. In *Proceedings of the International Conference RANLP-2009*, pages 144–149, Borovets, Bulgaria, September. Association for Computational Linguistics.

T. Hofmann. 1999. Probabilistic latent semantic indexing. In *Proceedings of the 22nd annual international ACM SIGIR conference on Research and development in information retrieval*, SIGIR '99, pages 50–57, New York, NY, USA. ACM.

K. Knight and D. Marcu. 2000. Statistics-Based Summarization – Step One: Sentence Compression. In *Proceedings of the Seventeenth National Conference on Artificial Intelligence and Twelfth Conference on Innovative Applications of Artificial Intelligence*, pages 703–710, Menlo Park, CA. AAAI Press.

W. Li, B. Li, and M. Wu. 2006. Query Focus Guided Sentence Selection Strategy.

C. Lin. 2004. ROUGE: A Package for Automatic Evaluation of Summaries. In *Proceedings of the Workshop on Text Summarization Branches Out (WAS 2004)*, pages 25–26. WAS 2004).

H. Luhn. 1958. The Automatic Creation of Literature Abstracts. *IBM Journal of Research and Development*, 2(2):159–165.

N. Madnani, D. Zajic, B. Dorr, N. Ayan, and J. Lin. 2007. Multiple Alternative Sentence Compressions for Automatic Text Summarization. In *Proceedings of the 7th Document Understanding Conference at NLT/NAACL*, page 26. DUC.

H. Morita, T. Sakai, and M. Okumura. 2011. Query Snowball: A Co-occurrence-based Approach to Multi-document Summarization for Question Answering. In *Proceedings of the 49th Annual Meeting of the Association for Computational Linguistics: Human Language Technologies: short papers - Volume 2*, HLT'11, pages 223–229, Stroudsburg, PA, USA. Association for Computational Linguistics.

A. Nenkova and L. Vanderwende. 2005. The impact of frequency on summarization. *Microsoft Research, Redmond, Washington, Tech. Rep. MSR-TR-2005-101*.

D. Radev, H. Jing, M. Sty, and D. Tam. 2004. Centroid-based Summarization of Multiple Documents. *Information Processing and Management*, 40:919–938.

P. Rayson and R. Garside. 2000. Comparing corpora using frequency profiling. In *Proceedings of the workshop on Comparing corpora - Volume 9*, WCC '00, pages 1–6, Stroudsburg, PA, USA.

P. Rayson, D. Berridge, and B. Francis. 2004. Extending the cochran rule for the comparison of word frequencies between corpora. In *Proceedings of the 7th International Conference on Statistical analysis of textual data (JADT 2004*, pages 926–936.

M. Scott. 2000. Focusing on the text and its key words. In *Burnard, L. and McEnery, T. (eds.) Rethinking language pedagogy from a corpus perspective: papers from the third international conference on teaching and language corpora*, pages 103–121.

Multilingual summarization system based on analyzing the discourse structure at MultiLing 2013

Daniel Alexandru Anechitei
"Al. I. Cuza" University of Iasi,
Faculty of Computer Science
16,General Berthelot St., 700483, Iasi,
Romania
daniel.anechitei@info.uaic.ro

Eugen Ignat
"Al. I. Cuza" University of Iasi,
Faculty of Computer Science
16,General Berthelot St., 700483, Iasi,
Romania
eugen.ignat@info.uaic.ro

Abstract

This paper describes the architecture of UAIC[1]'s Summarization system participating at MultiLing – 2013. The architecture includes language independent text processing modules, but also modules that are adapted for one language or another. In our experiments, the languages under consideration are Bulgarian, German, Greek, English, and Romanian. Our method exploits the cohesion and coherence properties of texts to build discourse structures. The output of the parsing process is used to extract general summaries.

1 Introduction

Automatic text summarization is a well studied research area and has been active for many years. In this paper, we describe the automatic text summarization system implemented by UAIC for participation at MultiLing 2013 single document track. Our approach to summarization follows the one presented in (Anechitei et al., 2013). The summarization architecture that this system uses includes two main parts that can be viewed in Figure 1. The text is passed to the language processing chain (LPC) which processes the data. As revealed from the figure each language has its own LPC. The LPC's, acts as a prerequisite for the summarization meta tool (SMT). In this paper we will focus more on the SMT engine, which is composed of four modules: anaphora resolution (AR), clause splitter (CS), discourse parser (DP) and the proper summarizer (SUM). The intermediate format between the modules consists of XML files. The summary of a text is obtained as a sequence of discourse clauses extracted from the original text, after obtaining the discourse structure of the text and exploiting the cohesion and coherence properties.

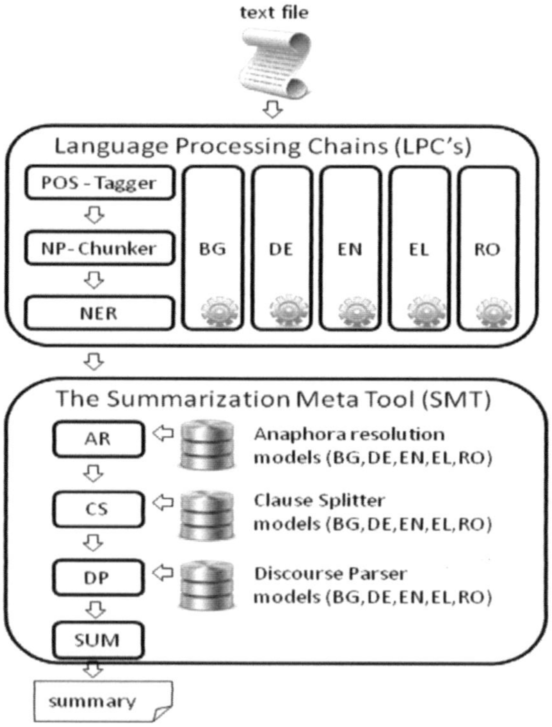

Figure 1: Summarization system architecture

2 Language Processing Chains

Every document is analyzed by the LPC in the following consecutive steps: sentence splitter, tokenizer, Part of Speech tagger, lemmatizer, Noun phrase extractor and Named entity recognizer. All tools are self-contained and designed

[1] University "Al. I. Cuza" of Iasi, Romania

to work in a chain, i.e. the output of the previous component is the input for the next component.

3 Anaphora Resolution

Anaphora resolution is one of the key steps of the discourse parser, by resolving anaphoric pronouns, automatically generated summaries may be more cohesive and, thus, more coherent. Calculating scores for references and transitions would be impossible without the proper identification of the co-referential chains.

Anaphora resolution is defined in (Orăsan et. al, 2008) as the process of resolving an anaphoric expression to the expression it refers to. The tool used for the anaphora resolution named RARE (Robust Anaphora Resolution Engine) uses the work done in (Cristea and Dima, 2001), where the process implies three layers (Figure 2):

- The text layer, containing referential expressions(RE) as they appear in the discourse;
- An intermediate layer (projection layer) that contains any specific information that can be extracted from the corresponding referential expressions.
- A semantic layer that contains descriptions of the discourse entities (DE). Here the information contributed by chains of referential expressions is accumulated.

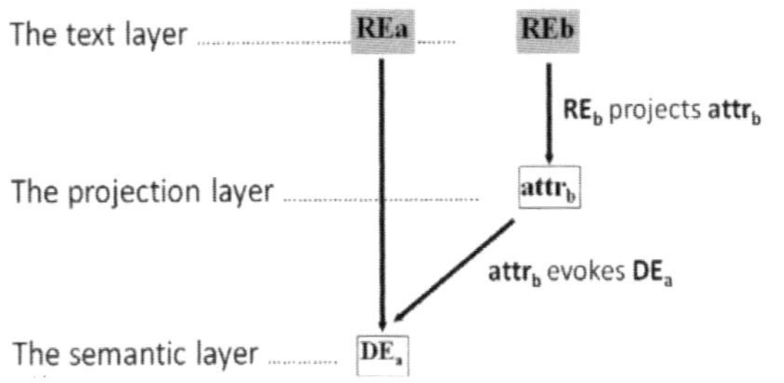

Figure 2: Three layers representation of co-referencing REs (Cristea and Dima, 2001)

The core of the system is language independent, but in order to localize it to one language or another it requires specific resources. These specific resources are as follows:

- **constraints** – containing the rules that match the conditions between anaphor and antecedent;
- **stopwords** – containing a list of stopwords;
- **tagset** – implies a mapping from the tagset used in the input file to a more simplified tagset used by the system.
- **window** – here is defined the length of the window where the antecedent should be looked for by the system.

The process of anaphora resolution runs as follows: The text is "read" from the left to right. When a new NP is found, a new RE is created and contains the morphological, syntactic and semantic features. All the features are tested using the constraints and it is decided whether the RE introduces a new discourse entity, not mentioned before, or it revokes one already mentioned.

4 Clause Splitter

Numerous techniques are used to recognize clause boundaries for different languages, where some are rule based (Leffa, 1988), and others are hybrid methods, like in (Parven et al., 2011) and (Orăsan, 2000), where the results of a machine learning algorithm, trained on an annotated corpus, are processed by a shallow rule-based module in order to improve the accuracy of the method. Our approach to discourse segmentation starts from the assumption that a clause is headed by a main verb, like "go" or a verbal compound, like "like to swim" (Ex.1). Verbs and verb compounds are considered pivots and clause boundaries are looked for in-between them.

Ex. 1 *<When I go to river>< I like to swim with my friends.>*

Verb compounds are sequences of more than one verb in which one is the main verb and the others are auxiliaries, infinitives, conjunctives that complement the main verb and the semantics of the main verb in context obliges to take the whole construction together. The CS module segments the input by applying a machine learning algorithm, to classify pairs of verbs as being or not compound verbs and, after that, applying rules and heuristics based on pattern matching or machine learning algorithms to identify the clause boundary. The exact place of a clause boundary between verbal phrases is best indicated by discourse markers. A discourse marker, like "because" (Ex.1), or, simply, marker, is a word or a group of words having the function to signal a clause boundary and/or to signal a rhetorical relation between two text spans.

Ex. 1 *<Markers are good><because they can give information on boundaries and discourse structure.>*

When markers are missing, boundaries are found by statistical methods, which are trained on explicit annotations given in manually built files. Based on the manually annotated files, a training module extracts two models (one for the CS module and one for the DP module). These models incorporate patterns of use of markers used to decide the segmentation boundaries and also to identify rhetorical relations between spans of text. The clauses act as terminal nodes in the process of discourse parsing which is described below.

5 Discourse Parser

Discourse parsing is the process of building a hierarchical model of a discourse from its basic elements (sentences or clauses), as one would build a parse of a sentence from its words (Bangalore and Stent, 2009). Rhetorical Structure Theory (Mann and Thompson, 1988) is one of the most popular discourse theories. In RST a text segment assumes one of two roles in a relationship: the nucleus (N) or satellite (S). Nuclei express what is more essential to the understanding of the narrative than the satellites. Our Discourse Parser uses a symbolic approach and produces discourse trees, which include nuclearity, but lacking rhetorical relation names: intermediate nodes in the discourse tree have no name and terminal nodes are elementary discourse units, mainly clauses. It adopts an incremental policy in developing the trees, on three levels (paragraphs, sentences and clauses) by consuming, recursively, one entire structure of an inferior level, by attaching the elementary discourse tree (*edt*) of the last structure to the already developed tree on the right frontier (Cristea and Webber, 1997). First, an *edt* of each sentence is produced using incremental parsing, by consuming each clause within the sentence. Secondly, the *edt* of the paragraph is produced by consuming each sentence within the paragraph. The same approach is used at discourse level by attaching the paragraph tree of each paragraph to the already developed tree. The criterion to guide the discourse parsing is represented by the principle of sequentiality (Marcu, 2000). The incremental discourse parsing approach borrows the two operations used in (L)TAG (*lexicalized tree-adjoining grammar*) (Joshi and Schabes, 1997): *adjunction* and *substitution*.

Adjunction operation (Figure 3) occurs only on the right frontier and it takes an initial or developing tree (D-tree_{i-1}), creating a new developing tree (D-tree_i) by combining D-tree_{i-1} with an auxiliary tree (A-tree), by replacing the *foot node* with the cropped tree. This is done for each node on the right frontier resulting in multiple D-trees. Figure 3 depicts this idea.

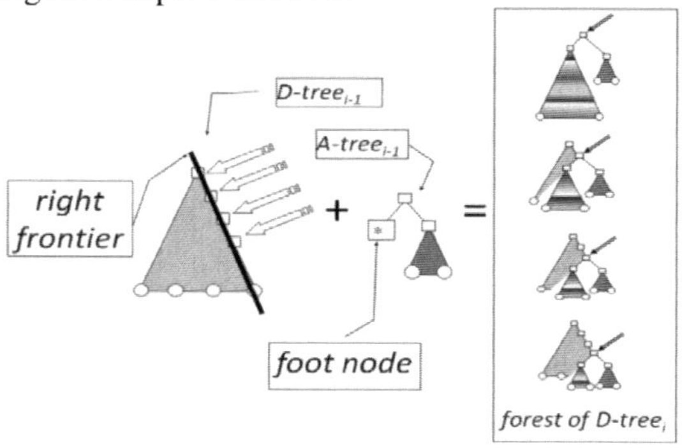

Figure 3: Adjunction operation

Substitution operation (Figure 4) replaces a placed node on a terminal frontier, called *substitution node*, with an auxiliary tree (Figure 14).

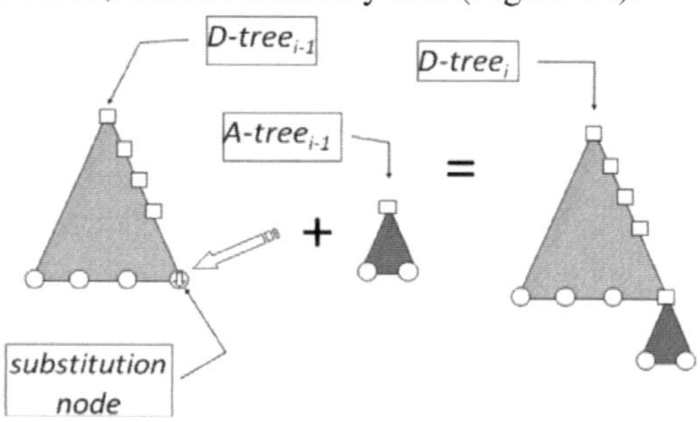

Figure 4: Substitution operation

The uses of different types of auxiliary trees (Figure 5) are determined by two factors:

- the type of operation in which are used: *alpha* and *beta* are used only for adjunction operations and *gamma* and *delta* for substitution operations;
- the auxiliary tree introduces or not an expectation: *beta* and *gamma* are auxiliary trees that raise an expectation and *alpha* an *delta* are auxiliary trees which do not raise an expectation.

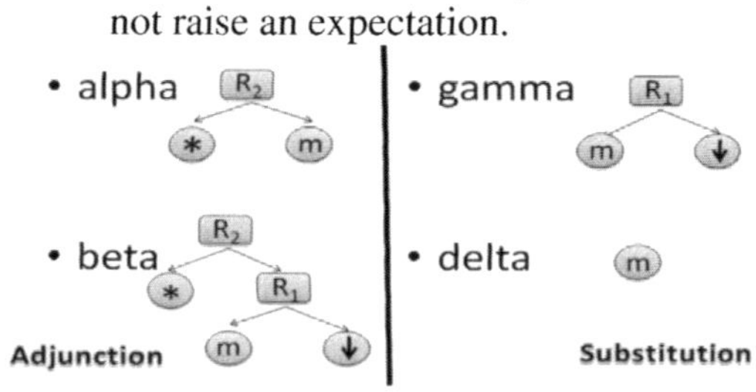

Figure 5: Types of auxiliary trees

At each parsing step there is a module which decides the type of the auxiliary tree between *alpha*, *gamma*, *beta*, *delta* (Anechitei et al., 2013) together with the relations type (R_1 and R_2, which can be N_N, N_S or S_N; the notation express the nuclearity of the child nodes: left one and the right one) by analyzing the structure which is processed (clause, sentence or paragraph). This module uses the compiled model described in previous section and doesn't produce a unique auxiliary tree for each structure but rather a set of trees.

At each level, the parser goes on with a forest of developing trees in parallel, ranking them by a global score (Figure 6) based on heuristics that are suggested by both Veins Theory (Cristea et al., 1998) and Centering Theory (Grosz et al., 1995). After normalizing the score for each heuristic, the global score is computed by summing the score of one heuristic with the corresponding weight. The weights were established after a calibration process.

$$GS^t = \sum_{i}^{N} s_i^h * w_i$$

Figure 6: Global score for each discourse tree

The trees used at the next step are only the best ranked trees. The aim of this filtering step is to reduce the exponential explosion of the obtained trees. For this task the threshold was set to *five best trees* from iteration to another and six (N=6) heuristics chosen in a way to maximize the coherence of the discourse structure and implicitly the coherence of the summary.

6 The Summarizer

The mentioned system produces excerpt type summaries, which are summaries that copy contiguous sequences of tokens from the original text.

The structure of a discourse as a complete tree gives more information than properly needed (at least for summarization purpose). By exploiting the discourse structure, we expect to add cohesion and coherence to our summaries. From the discourse structure we can extract three types of summaries: general summaries, entity focused summaries and clause focused summaries. For the summarization task we only extracted the general summary. The module that extracts the summaries (SUM) takes the tree of a discourse structure and produces a general summary, of a certain length, depending on the length of the computed vein (Cristea et al., 1998). As the task supposed summaries containing a maximum of 250 words and the summaries the system was providing were always bigger, a new scoring system was needed. This scoring system needed to shorten the summaries to under 250 words, yet keep as much coherence and cohesion as the system provided. For this end the scoring system took all the clauses from the vein and scored them as follows: in each clause the noun phrases were found, for each noun phrase a coreferential score was given. These scores are added and computed for each clause. The clauses were sorted and only the first N clauses were selected such as the maximum coherence was retained, where N is the number of the clauses so that the final summaries are below the word count threshold. The score for each noun phrase is given taking into account how big the coreference chain is.

7 Conclusion and Results

This year, the evaluation at MultiLing 2013 was performed automatically using N-gram graph methods, which were interchangeable in the single document setting. Below we provide the results based on average NPowER grades.

Lang	UAIC	Mary-land (I)	Mary-land (II)	Mary-land (II)	Baseline
BG	1.538	1.600	1.593	1.600	1.310
DE	1.537	1.64	1.612	1.617	1.289
EL	1.560	1.501	1.513	1.494	1.314
EN	1.646	1.641	1.661	1.656	1.367
RO	1.627	1.655	1.679	1.680	1.346
	1.582	**1.607**	**1.611**	**1.609**	**1.325**

Table 1: Table with results

Table 1 shows the comparison between UAIC's system and Maryland's system, as it was the only other system, besides the baseline, that ran on the same 5 languages. Generally the results of both systems are close as the average figure shows. For our first participation the results are encouraging for this complex system, which has the possibility of running on multiple languages. Our future work should reside in the scorer of the summarizer, as the approach usually creates summaries bigger than 250 words.

References

Anechitei A. Daniel, Cristea Dan, Dimosthenis Ioannidis, Ignat Eugen, Karagiozov Diman, Koeva Svetla, Kopeć Mateusz and Vertan Cristina. 2013. *Summarizing Short Texts Through a Discourse-Centered Approach in a Multilingual Context*. In Neustein, A., Markowitz, J.A. (eds.), Where Humans Meet Machines: Innovative Solutions to Knotty Natural Language Problems. Springer Verlag, Heidelberg/New York.

Bangalore Srinivas and Stent J. Amanda. 2009. *Incremental parsing models for dialog task structure*, in Proceedings of the 12th Conference of the European Chapter of the Association for Computational Linguistics.

Cristea Dan and Webber Bonnie. 1997. *Expectations in incremental discourse processing*. In Proceedings of the 8th Conference of the European Chapter of the Association for Computational Linguistics.

Cristea Dan, Ide Nancy and Romary Laurent. 1998: Veins Theory: A Model of Global Discourse Cohesion and Coherence, in Proceedings of the 17th international conference on Computational linguistics.

Cristea Dan and Dima E. Gabriela. 2001. *An integrating framework for anaphora resolution*. In Information Science and Technology, Romanian Academy Publishing House, Bucharest, vol. 4, no. 3-4, p 273-291.

Grosz J. Barbara, Joshi K. Arvind and Weinstein Scott. 1995. *Centering: A Framework for Modelling the Local Coherence of Discourse*. Computational Linguistics, 21/2: 203-25.

Joshi K. Aravind and Schabes Yves. 1997: *Tree-Adjoining Grammars*. In G. Rozenberg and A.Salomaa, editors, Handbook of Formal languages.

Leffa J. Vilson. 1988. *Clause processing in complex sentences*. In Proceedings of the First International Conference on Language Resource and Evaluation, volume 1, pages 937 – 943, May 1998.

Mann C. William and Thompson A. Sandra. 1988. *Rhetorical structure theory: a theory of text organization*. Text 8(3):243–281.

Marcu Daniel. 2000. *The Theory and Practice of Discourse Parsing and Summarization*. The MIT Press, November 2000.

Orasan Constantin. 2000. *A hybrid method for clause splitting in unrestricted English texts*. In Proceedings of ACIDCA, Corpora and Natural Language Processing, March 22-24, Monastir, Tunisia, pp. 129 – 134.

Orăsan Constantin, Cristea Dan, Mitkov Ruslan and Branco Antonio. 2008. *Anaphora Resolution Exercise – An Overview*. In Proceedings of LREC-2008, Marrakech, Morocco.

Parveen Daraksha, Sanyal Ratna and Ansari Afreen. 2011. *Clause Boundary Identification using Classifier and Clause Markers in Urdu Language*. Polibits Research Journal on Computer Science, 43, pp. 61-65.

Multilingual Single-Document Summarization with MUSE

Marina Litvak
Department of Software Engineering
Shamoon College of Engineering
Beer Sheva, Israel
marinal@sce.ac.il

Mark Last
Department of Information Systems
Engineering, Ben Gurion University
Beer Sheva, Israel
mlast@bgu.ac.il

Abstract

MUltilingual Sentence Extractor (MUSE) is aimed at multilingual single-document summarization. MUSE implements a supervised language-independent summarization approach based on optimization of multiple sentence ranking methods using a Genetic Algorithm. The main advantage of MUSE is its language-independency – it is using statistical sentence features, which can be calculated for sentences in any language.

In our previous work, the performance of MUSE was found to be significantly better than the best known state-of-the-art extractive summarization approaches and tools in three different languages: English, Hebrew, and Arabic. Moreover, our experimental results in the cross-lingual domain suggest that MUSE does not need to be retrained on a summarization corpus in each new language, and the same weighting model can be used across several languages (Last and Litvak, 2012).

MUSE participated in the MultiLing 2013 single document summarization task on three languages: English, Hebrew and Arabic. Due to a very limited time that was given to the participants to run their systems on the MultiLing 2013 data, the results submitted to evaluation were obtained by summarizing the documents using models *pre-trained* on *different* corpora. As such, no training has been performed on the MultiLing 2013 corpus.

1 MUltilingual Sentence Extractor (MUSE): Overview

1.1 Methodology

MUSE implements a *supervised* learning approach to language-independent extractive summarization where the best set of weights for a linear combination of sentence scoring methods is found by a genetic algorithm trained on a collection of documents and their summaries. The weighting vector thus obtained is used for sentence scoring in future summarizations. Since most sentence scoring methods have a linear computational complexity, only the training phase of our approach is time-consuming.

Using MUSE, the user can choose the subset of totally 31 sentence metrics that will be included in the linear combination. The available metrics are based on various text representation models and are language-independent since they do not rely on any language-specific knowledge. Figure 1 demonstrates the taxonomy of all 31 metrics. We divided them into three main categories—*structure*-, *vector*-, and *graph*-based—according to their text representation model, where each subcategory contains group of metrics using the same scoring method.

A detailed description of sentence metrics used by MUSE can be found in (Last and Litvak, 2012).

The best linear combination of the metrics depicted in Figure 1 can be found using a Genetic Algorithm (GA). GAs are categorized as global search heuristics. Figure 2 shows a simplified GA flowchart.

A typical genetic algorithm requires (1) a genetic representation of the solution domain, (2) a fitness function to evaluate the solution domain, and (3) some basic parameter settings like selection and reproduction rules.

We represent each solution as a vector of weights for a linear combination of sentence scor-

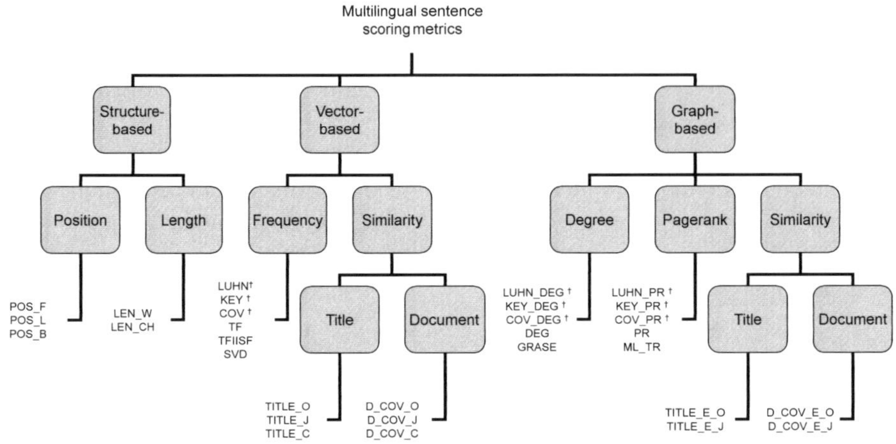

Figure 1: Taxonomy of language-independent sentence scoring metrics (Litvak et al., 2010b)

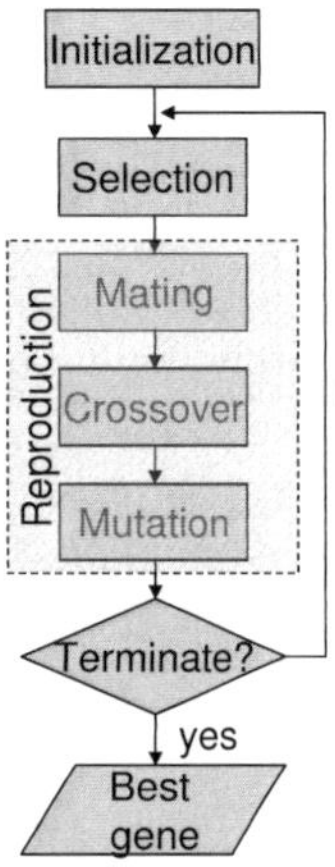

Figure 2: Simplified flowchart of GA

Algorithm 1 Step 1: Training

Require: Gold Standard - a corpus of summarized documents D, N chosen metrics
Ensure: A weighted model W - vector of weights for each of N metrics
  Step 1.1: Compute M - sentence-score matrix
  for all $d \in D$ **do**
    Let R_1, R_2, and R_3 are d representations
    for all sentences $s \in d$ **do**
      Calculate N metrics using R_1, R_2, and R_3
      Add metrics row for s into M
    end for
  end for
  Step 1.2: Compute a vector W of metrics weights
  Run a Genetic Algorithm on M, given D:
  Initialize a population P
  repeat
    for all solution $g \in P$ **do**
      Generate a summary a
      Evaluate a by ROUGE on summaries of D
    end for
    Select the best solutions G
    P - a new population generated by G
  until convergence - no better solutions are found
  return a vector W of weights - output of a GA

ing metrics—real-valued numbers in the unlimited range normalized in such a way that they sum up to 1. The vector size is fixed and it equals to the number of metrics used in the combination.

Defined over the genetic representation, the fitness function measures the quality of the represented solution. We can use ROUGE-1 and ROUGE-2, Recall (Lin and Hovy, 2003) as a fitness functions for measuring summarization quality—similarity with gold standard summaries, which should be *maximized* during the training (optimization procedure). We use an annotated corpus of summarized documents, where each document is accompanied by several human-generated summaries—abstracts or extracts, as a training set.

The reader is referred to (Litvak et al., 2010b) for a detailed description of the optimization procedure implemented by MUSE.

Algorithms 1 and 2 contain the pseudo-code for two independent phases of MUSE: training and summarization, respectively. Assuming efficient implementation, all metrics have a linear computational complexity relative to the total number of words in a document - $O(n)$. As a result, the summary extraction time, given a trained model, is also linear (in the number of metrics in a combination). The training time is proportional to the number of GA iterations multiplied by the number of individuals in a population times the fitness evaluation (ROUGE) time. On average, in our experiments the GA performed $5 - 6$ iterations—

Algorithm 2 Step 2: Summarizing a new document

Require: A document d, maximal summary length L, a trained weighted model W
Ensure: A set of n sentences, which were top-ranked by the algorithm as the most important.
  Step 2.1: Compute a score of each sentence
  Let R_1, R_2, and R_3 are d representations
  for all sentense $s \in d$ **do**
    Calculate N metrics using R_1, R_2, and R_3
    Calculate a score as a linear combination according to W
  end for
  Step 2.2: Compile the document summary
  Let $S = \emptyset$ be a summary of d
  repeat
    get the top ranked sentence s_i
    $S = S \bigcup s_i$
  until S exceeds max length L
  return S

selection and reproduction—before reaching convergence.

1.2 Architecture

The current version of MUSE tool can be applied only to text documents or textual content of HTML pages. It consists of two main modules: the *training module* activated in offline, and the real-time *summarization module*. Both modules utilize two different representations of documents described in (Litvak et al., 2010b): vector- and graph-based. The *preprocessing module* is responsible for constructing each representation, and it is embedded in both modules.

The *training module* receives as input a corpus of documents, each accompanied by one or several gold-standard summaries—abstracts or extracts—compiled by human assessors. The set of documents may be either monolingual or multilingual and their summaries have to be in the same language as the original text. The *training module* applies a genetic algorithm to a document-feature matrix of precomputed sentence scores with the purpose of finding the best linear combination of features using any ROUGE metric as a fitness function. ROUGE-1 Recall is used as a default unless specified otherwise by the end-user. The output/model of the training module is a vector of weights for user-specified sentence ranking features. In the current version of the tool, the user can choose from 31 vector-based and graph-based features. The recommendation for the best 10 features can be found in (Litvak et al., 2010a).

The *summarization module* performs summarization of input text/texts in real time. Each sentence of an input text obtains a relevance score according to the trained model, and the top ranked sentences are extracted to the summary in their original order. The length of resulting summaries is limited by a user-specified value (maximum number of words, maximum number of sentences or a compression ratio). Being activated in real-time, the *summarization module* is expected to use the model trained on the same language as input texts. However, if such model is not available (no annotated corpus in the text language), the user can choose one of the following options: (1) a model trained on some other language/corpus (in (Litvak et al., 2010b) we show that the same model can be efficiently used across different languages), or (2) user-specified weights for each sentence feature (from 31 provided in the system) in the linear combination.

The *preprocessing module* performs the following tasks: (1) sentence segmentation, (2) word segmentation, (3) vector space model construction using *tf* and/or *tf-idf* weights, (4) a word-based graph representation construction, (5) a sentence-based graph representation construction, and (6) document metadata construction, including such information like frequency (tf and tf-idf) for each unique term, its location inside the document, etc. The outputs of this submodule are: sentence segmented text (SST), vector space model (VSM), the document graphs, and the metadata stored in the xml files. Steps (1) and (2) are performed by the *text processor submodule*, which consists of three elements: *filter*, *reader* and *sentence segmenter*. The *filter* works on the Unicode character level and performs such operations like identification of characters, digits, punctuations and normalization (optional for some languages). The *reader* invokes the *filter*, constructs word chunks from the input stream and identifies the following states: *words, special characters, white spaces, numbers, URL links* and *punctuation marks*. The *sentence segmenter* invokes *reader* and divides the input space into sentences. By implementing different filters, the reader can work either with a specific language (taking into account its intricacies) or with documents written in arbitrary language (in this case, a general filtering according to UTF-8 encoding is performed).

Figure 3 shows the general architecture of the MUSE system.

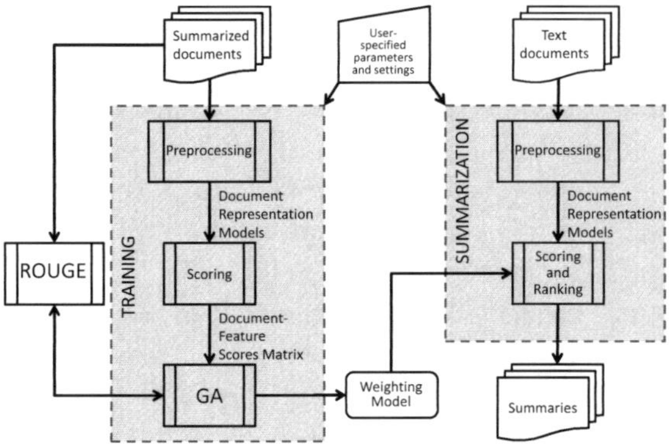

Figure 3: MUSE architecture

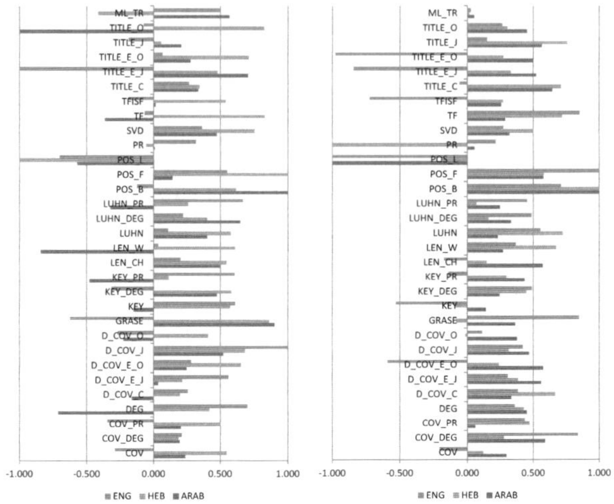

Figure 4: Models trained on monolingual corpora: ROUGE-1 (left) and ROUGE-2 (right)

2 Training of MUSE

Since a very limited time was given to participants to run their summarizers on the MultiLing 2013 dataset, we did not perform training on a new data. The models obtained from training MUSE on monolingual corpora of English, Hebrew, and Arabic texts in 2011 (Last and Litvak, 2012), have been used for summarization in three languages. Both ROUGE-1 and ROUGE-2 have beed used for building the models. In the current settings, ROUGE-1-based models were utilized.

The English text material used in the experiments comprised the corpus of summarized documents available for the summarization task at the Document Understanding Conference 2002 (DUC, 2002). This benchmark dataset contains 533 news articles, each accompanied by two to three human-generated *abstracts* of approximately 100 words each.

For the Arabic language, we used a corpus compiled from 90 news articles. Each article was summarized by three native Arabic speakers selecting the most important sentences into an *extractive* summary of approximately 100 words each.

For the Hebrew language, we used a corpus where 120 news articles of 250 to 830 words are summarized by five human assessors each.

The documents from all corpora have a title as the first sentence.

ROUGE-1 and ROUGE-2 metrics (Lin, 2004) have been used as a fitness function during the training of MUSE. The same metrics have been used for evaluation of generated summaries in three languages. In order to use the ROUGE toolkit on Hebrew and Arabic, it was adapted to these languages by specifying the regular expressions for a single "word" using Hebrew and Arabic characters.

Figure 4 present models learned by MUSE on different monolingual corpora using ROUGE-1 and ROUGE-2, respectively. The actual results in the trained models include some negative values.

The evaluation results of MUSE on three monolingual corpora using 10-fold cross validation showed its significant superiority over *TextRank* (Mihalcea, 2005), the best known language-independent unsupervised approach.

3 Experimental Results

According to the results of automated evaluation in MultiLing 2013 (N-gram graph methods: AutoSummENG, MeMoG, NPowER), MUSE took **fourth** place in English corpus (out of 7 systems), **third** place in Hebrew (out of 5 summarizers), and the **first** place in Arabic (out of 6 participants). We believe, that training MUSE on the original data and using correct titles[1] (by parsing xml documents) may significantly improve its results.

[1] Due to the time constraints of the single-document summarization task, we used a simple txt format of summarized documents in the published dataset, where the title is not separated from the first sentence by punctuation marks.

References

DUC. 2002. Document Understanding Conference. http://duc.nist.gov.

M. Last and M. Litvak. 2012. Cross-lingual training of summarization systems using annotated corpora in a foreign language. *Information Retrieval*, pages 1–28, September.

Chin-Yew Lin and Eduard Hovy. 2003. Automatic evaluation of summaries using N-gram co-occurrence statistics. In *NAACL '03: Proceedings of the 2003 Conference of the North American Chapter of the Association for Computational Linguistics on Human Language Technology*, pages 71–78.

Chin-Yew Lin. 2004. ROUGE: A Package for Automatic Evaluation of summaries. In *Proceedings of the Workshop on Text Summarization Branches Out (WAS 2004)*, pages 25–26.

M. Litvak, S. Kisilevich, D. Keim, H. Lipman, A. Ben-Gur, and M. Last. 2010a. Towards language-independent summarization: A comparative analysis of sentence extraction methods on english and hebrew corpora. In *Proceedings of the CLIA/COLING 2010*.

Marina Litvak, Mark Last, and Menahem Friedman. 2010b. A new approach to improving multilingual summarization using a Genetic Algorithm. In *ACL '10: Proceedings of the 48th Annual Meeting of the Association for Computational Linguistics*, pages 927–936.

Rada Mihalcea. 2005. Language independent extractive summarization. In *AAAI'05: Proceedings of the 20th National Conference on Artificial Intelligence*, pages 1688–1689.

Author Index

Association for Computational Linguistics
209 N. Eighth Street
Stroudsburg, Pennsylvania 18360

CURRAN ASSOCIATES INC
proceedings.com